THE GREAT MANAGEMENT RESET

I first met Leslie Kaminoff about twenty-two years ago when I was a young associate lawyer. Over the years, I have worked hand-in-hand with Leslie as he transformed his successful property management company into AKAM Living Services Inc. (ALSI), a family of real estate enterprises in New York and South Florida. ALSI's entities are experts at minimizing operating costs while maximizing property value. Of course, no one can accomplish this type of success all on their own. By focusing on hiring competent, intelligent employees and training them in the programs he designed, Leslie has created a workforce with a strong focus on excellence in customer service. As a result, he has simultaneously built a hugely successful enterprise and developed a reputation for delivering on his promises.

Today, the AKAM I once knew as successful has more than quadrupled in size and profitability—and it shows no signs of slowing down! I greatly trust Leslie's expertise in the management of his employees. He has truly earned his reputation for excellence in customer service.

—Robert Lesser, Esq.

"Visionary" is one of the words I would use to best describe Leslie Kaminoff. I have known Leslie both personally and professionally for over twenty-five years. About ten years ago he saw the need to assist his management clients in the numerous capital improvement projects they were undertaking, so he formed Project Management Group, an ALSI company, which has grown to be a major player in both the New York and Florida markets.

I have watched Leslie become both a respected voice in the NY real estate community and a game changer in the Florida market, where he transformed the property management industry. During my association with him I have seen the personal side of him as well. His commitment to his employees is remarkable, borne out by the number that have been with him in excess of twenty years, during which time he has been both mentor and friend to them and their families. It is an honor and a privilege to continue to be associated with Leslie and his companies.

—**Doug Weinstein**, Vice President, PMG Inc.

THE GREAT
MANAGEMENT
RESET

27 Ways to be a Better Manager
(of Anything)

Leslie Kaminoff

New York

THE GREAT MANAGEMENT RESET
27 Ways to be a Better Manager (of Anything)

© 2017 Leslie Kaminoff.

Published in New York, New York, by Morgan James Publishing. Morgan James and The Entrepreneurial Publisher are trademarks of Morgan James, LLC. www.MorganJamesPublishing.com

The Morgan James Speakers Group can bring authors to your live event. For more information or to book an event visit The Morgan James Speakers Group at www.TheMorganJamesSpeakersGroup.com.

Shelfie

A free eBook edition is available with the purchase of this print book.

CLEARLY PRINT YOUR NAME ABOVE IN UPPER CASE

Instructions to claim your free eBook edition:
1. Download the Shelfie app for Android or iOS
2. Write your name in **UPPER CASE** above
3. Use the Shelfie app to submit a photo
4. Download your eBook to any device

ISBN 978-1-63047-915-2 paperback
ISBN 978-1-63047-916-9 eBook
ISBN 978-1-63047-917-6 hardcover
Library of Congress Control Number:
2015920737

Cover Design by:
Chris Treccani
www.3dogdesign.net

Interior Design by:
Bonnie Bushman
The Whole Caboodle Graphic Design

In an effort to support local communities and raise awareness and funds, Morgan James Publishing donates a percentage of all book sales for the life of each book to Habitat for Humanity Peninsula and Greater Williamsburg

Get involved today, visit
www.MorganJamesBuilds.com

Habitat for Humanity®
Peninsula and
Greater Williamsburg
Building Partner

I dedicate this book
to my wife Kimberly, and my children,
Alexis, Ashley, and Justin.
Thank you for all your support throughout the years.

CONTENTS

ACKNOWLEDGMENTS

First and foremost, I would like to thank my wife, Kimberly, as well as my three lovely children, Alexis, Ashley, and Justin. Many hours have gone into organizing my thoughts and transcribing them to paper. Through it all, my family has been supportive and encouraging. They are continually there for me through the hard times and the achievements, and I can't thank them enough for their support during this process.

Additionally, I have been blessed to be surrounded and supported by some of the most creative, effective, and hardworking executives. From these team members, I have learned much. They are a courageous group that embraces challenges and are not afraid to think and perform outside the box. What I have learned from them is boundless. This also leads me to thank the Stony Brook University Music faculty and class of 1977 for inspiring **Bonus Chapter 2**, my speech to Stony Brook's School of Music 2011 graduates.

And of course, thank you to my publisher, Morgan James Publishing, for supporting this project from start to finish. As well, thank you to my editor, Angie Kiesling of The Editorial Attic, for assisting me in the presentation of my thoughts on this topic.

Pre-read Management Self-Survey

Welcome to *The Great Management Reset* Pre-read Management Self-Survey.

Below are twenty-seven statements, all drawn from the messages in this book. Read each statement and then circle the number that best fits how well you agree with the statement. Add your total at the end.

Never	Sometimes	Often	Almost always	Always
1	2	3	4	5

1. I understand what the people on my management team really want from me.

1	2	3	4	5

2. I am able to engage the members of my management team so they are optimally productive.

    1   2   3   4   5

3. I am fully and openly accountable to the people on my management team.

    1   2   3   4   5

4. I am able to prioritize my tasks and projects easily and quickly.

    1   2   3   4   5

5. I know how to set realistic task and project management goals.

    1   2   3   4   5

6.   I have a management plan and a backup plan for each task and project.

    1   2   3   4   5

7. I feel confident about meeting management deadlines.

    1   2   3   4   5

8. I use to-do lists and action lists to manage my time.

    1   2   3   4   5

9. I manage my time so that I have enough time to do my own work.

   1   2   3   4   5

10. My management plans target maximum profitability.

   1   2   3   4   5

11. I maximize the value of my management and my management team.

   1   2   3   4   5

12. I am able to deliver management tasks and projects on budget.

   1   2   3   4   5

13. I use communication effectively to keep my management team on track.

   1   2   3   4   5

14. I am able to make problems productive.

   1   2   3   4   5

15. I conduct worthwhile meetings.

   1   2   3   4   5

16. I deliver excellent management service to my supervisors.

   1   2   3   4   5

17. I deliver excellent management service to my management team members.

    1   2   3   4   5

18. I deliver excellent management service to the consumers (clients or customers) of my organization.

    1   2   3   4   5

19. I have clearly articulated my own values as a manager.

    1   2   3   4   5

20. I am consistent in the way I manage and in the results I achieve.

    1   2   3   4   5

21. I understand how to enhance my own reputation as a manager.

    1   2   3   4   5

22. I understand what happens to people and organizations during change.

    1   2   3   4   5

23. I know how to plan for and execute change.

    1   2   3   4   5

24. I know how to manage change so my management team members embrace the new normal.

    1   2   3   4   5

25. I take stock of myself regularly.

    1   2   3   4   5

26. I know how to manage stress in my own life.

    1   2   3   4   5

27. I manage my life so that I can enjoy myself.

    1   2   3   4   5

Pre-read Management Self-Survey Total _____

Management must manage!
—Harold S. Geneen, Former CEO of ITT

LESLIE'S PERSPECTIVE: THE GREAT MANAGEMENT RESET

What do you manage? Do you manage a business, a department, or a project? Do you manage a team, a household, or an organization? Whatever it is you manage, I know from experience that it's easier to manage when you have the guidance and insight of those who have successfully walked the path before you.

As an expert in the field of management I believe I have much to contribute. Frankly, there's a lot of misinformation out there about what good management is and what it's supposed to do. It's time to take a step back, look at the realities of management, and cut through the noise to examine what really works.

In other words, it's time for *The Great Management Reset*.

And why am I qualified to make such a bold claim? This is my background: As founder and CEO of AKAM Living Services Inc. (ALSI), I have overseen eight real estate service companies operating in New York and Florida since 1983. Among the ALSI companies are AKAM Associates and AKAM On-Site, award-winning leaders in the New York and South Florida residential management arenas, and The Ashtin Group, an innovator in the management of commercial and educational facilities. For over thirty years I have managed the assets of tens of thousands of clients while simultaneously managing the growth of multiple companies employing more than fifteen hundred employees. Recently *SmartCEO* magazine named me Chief Executive Officer of the Year, among other awards and recognitions from within and outside the management industry.

I coauthored a book titled *How to Choose the Right Management Company*; created and facilitated the AKAM Residential Management Professional training program, the first company-specific credential in the industry; and developed the AKAM Excellence Academy, which provides ongoing educational opportunities to all ALSI employees in addition to presenting seminars and classes that are open to the public.

With the debut of *The Great Management Reset*, my goal is to pull back the curtain on management, ease the path for those who manage on the front lines, elevate the practice of management, and cultivate the next generation of management leaders.

Let's start the reset with the only useful response I've seen to the question "What is management?" The simple but all-encompassing answer offers the advice, information, and intelligence on the forthcoming pages. Basically:

Management is the identification, organization, deployment, and control of available resources to accomplish a stated goal.

As a manager—of anything—a goal is presented and your job is to identify, organize, deploy, and control your available resources to accomplish that goal. That's it, and that's a lot. Anything anyone else tells you about management is just so much fluff added to make management seem more challenging than it already is. And as you know, it's already challenging enough.

You will find this book very easy to read. Thoughts are organized into nine categories of management with three perspectives explained in each category, complete with how-to lists and questions to encourage you to reset your own understanding and practice of management.

My goal is to help you see clearly both the science and the art of management so you can operate with greater confidence and success in the areas of People Management, Task and Project Management, Time Management, Money Management, Communication Management, Service Management, Reputation Management, Change Management, and Self- Management.

As you progress in the book, I address and answer such persistent management questions as: What do the people you manage really want from you? How do you decide what to do and when to do it? How do you manage deadlines? How do you manage within a budget? How can you make problems productive? How can you deliver service to your own management team? How can you enhance your reputation as a manager? How do you plan for and execute change? How can you manage the stress that management brings and also manage to enjoy yourself?

To help you see how much you will grow between the time you start and finish *The Great Management Reset*, I've included a pre-read and post-read survey. Any change for the positive is management growth you should celebrate. I'm confident that you will continue to grow as a manager each time you refer to this book.

I've also included a bonus chapter at the end of the book. This chapter on leadership and management discusses the next step in *The Great Management Reset*. It presents the position that while not all leaders must be managers, all managers must be leaders. Its purpose is to encourage you to become a management leader and to share your strength with those who can benefit from it, just as I hope I have done for you.

Now, let's begin *The Great Management Reset*.

People Management

The great myth is the manager as orchestra conductor. It's this idea of standing on a pedestal and you wave your baton and accounting comes in, and you wave it somewhere else and marketing chimes in with accounting, and they all sound very glorious.

~

But management is more like orchestra conducting during rehearsals, when everything is going wrong.
—**Henry Mintzberg**, International management expert, author, and educator

~

In the opening pages, I established that management is the identification, organization, deployment, and control of available resources to achieve a stated goal. Here's where people fit into all that.

People are the world's most valuable resources. Nothing can be accomplished without people. Even if you think you can manage all by yourself without help from anyone else (which, by the way, you can't), if there's no one on the other end to receive the product of your efforts, then what you do has no context, no meaning, and no value. Without the context, meaning, and value that people contribute and attribute to management, management amounts to nothing.

It would be divine if your most valuable management resources were also the easiest of all resources to identify, organize, deploy, and control. But that's not how the world works. It's certainly not how people work.

If you've ever identified the "perfect" candidate only to discover that you made a real whopper in terms of judging character or competence ...

If you've ever tried to organize a group of thinking adults into a cohesive team with a single purpose ...

If you've ever deployed individuals and teams to perform independently and report back truthfully and completely ...

If you've ever tried to control any number of people, in any situation ...

Then you know that *people* are the most difficult of all resources to manage.

No surprise. After all, people are independent beings who are wired to process, respond to, and participate in what happens to them and around them.

Yet as a manager (of anything), managing people is what you must do.

So what's the best way to approach managing people?

I think you'll be way ahead of the game if you reset your management approach so that you:

1. Know what people really want from you as a manager.
2. Know how to engage your people and get them on board.
3. Model accountability by being accountable to the people you manage.

1. What the People You Manage Really Want from You

~

So much of what we call management consists in making it difficult for people to work.

—**Peter Drucker**, Renowned management
thought leader, educator, and author

~

Here's what the people you manage really want from you. And this is true whether you're managing a work cohort, a family unit, a sports team, or a tour group.

The people you manage want you to make things easy for them.

Does that sound like managing for slackers? On the contrary. The fact is, most people want to do a good job, feel part of the clan, contribute to a winning game, or participate in seeing the world. They're willing to put in the effort ... but something is standing in their way.

I'm suggesting that you reset your understanding of people management by identifying variables that may be obstacles for the people you're managing and then removing those obstacles. You can do this in the following ways:

1. **Clear expectations, purpose, and goals.** People need to know what you expect of them, what their purpose is, and what they're working toward. Give it to them in writing.
2. **A sense of the bigger picture.** People need to know where they fit into the overall goal. Take the time to explain to them the importance of their contribution.
3. **Feedback and communication.** People need to know how they're doing so they know whether or not they're on the right track and what they need to do to adjust their direction for success. Schedule and hold regular feedback and information sessions.

4. **Positive reinforcement.** People do not respond well to management that manages by looking for mistakes. Negative reinforcement breeds negative performance. On the other hand, positive reinforcement yields powerfully positive results. Make an effort to catch people when they do something right. Remember: Praise in public.

5. **Respect.** It's people you're dealing with here, and they deserve the basics of human respect. That means reasonable work conditions, prompt response to questions and requests for your help, and the expectation that you're not going to throw them under the bus or threaten to fire them every time things don't go exactly as planned. You also need to respect the fact that they have a personal life outside of your realm of management. Rule of thumb: Don't be a jerk. And remember, discipline in private (with a witness, as necessary).

6. **Challenges and opportunities.** People respond best when they're encouraged—and given opportunities—to stretch and to shine. Give these to your people and they will produce.

7. **Consistency.** People have a right to expect to be treated the same as everyone else. You can have your favorites (come on, it's only human)—just don't show it.

8. **Loyalty.** Show the people you manage that you have their backs. This is a deposit in the bank that they will then be more inclined to do the same for you.

9. **Fair and equal compensation.** People need to be paid fairly. All people doing the same job should be paid the same amount. No one should have to ask for this—it should be baked in the cake.

10. **You as a role model.** Manage as a role model of engagement and accountability, and the people you manage will be likely to echo your standard.

The Great Management Reset: What the People You Manage Really Want from You

- How do you respond to the truth that the people you manage want you to make it easy for them to give you what you need? Do you agree that managing for ease of performance is your responsibility? Why or why not?

- Do you believe that removing obstacles to performance is, or is not, within your management power? If not, what needs to change? How can you bring about this change?

- Review my list of ten ways to give the people you manage what they want. Do you agree with everything on the list? With what do you disagree?

Why? What needs to happen for you to agree with all the items on the list?

- How would resetting your people management skills impact your professional life? Your personal life? Your other activities?
- What can you do immediately to reset and improve your people management? What's stopping you?

2. How to Engage Your People

∼

It goes without saying that no company, small or large, can win over the long run without energized employees who believe in the mission and understand how to achieve it.

—**Jack Welch**, Former CEO of GE

∼

There's a lot of talk these days about engagement—engagement at work, engagement in families, engagement in the world at large.

What I mean when I talk about engagement is the commitment to a common vision, the motivation to contribute to the fulfillment of that vision, and a positive feeling of productivity and satisfaction when that commitment and motivation are activated. Engagement is the involvement of people's hearts and minds in what needs to be accomplished at work, at home, or in whatever situation.

The not-so-good news is this: A recent Gallup poll reveals that 55 percent of workplace employees are not engaged in their work. That's more than half of all workers who basically are doing the least they can do without getting fired.

In contrast, engaged individuals arrive on time and willingly stay until their work is done. They express pride in their job. They take ownership of their assignments, go above and beyond in the performance of what is expected of them, and volunteer to perform additional responsibilities. They demonstrate a desire to grow into a higher level of participation.

Obviously, engaged individuals will accomplish more, and do so more eagerly than those who are not engaged.

I'm suggesting that you make it part of your management mission to maximize engagement among the people you manage.

You can do this by activating the last section's list of ten ways to give the people you manage what they want, and by incorporating these additional five ways to increase the level of engagement among the people you manage:

1. **Provide a mission statement and statement of values.** A clarified mission and a specific list of values

will identify what your group is about and what principles inform your activities. These statements let people know what they're being asked to fully engage in and they clarify what success is supposed to look like.

2. **Invest in your people.** Give your people the equipment and support they need to produce their own best results. Expose them to best practices so they're not stuck reinventing the wheel. And train them so they know what they're doing and can focus on the bigger picture.

3. **Cultivate a culture and a community.** This makes people feel "a part of" instead of "apart from." Develop habits and practices unique to your group. Provide regular updates in writing and in-group meetings. Host public acknowledgments and group celebrations. Hold events so your team can interact socially with each other.

4. **Be open to innovation and passion.** Encourage and welcome the next great idea from the people you manage. Let no well-intentioned idea ever be labeled stupid or unworthy.

5. **Make excellence and extraordinary performance the standard.** This means you must set the bar and be the role model of expectations and performance for the people you manage.

The Great Management Reset:
How to Engage Your People

- Think about a time when you should have been engaged in something but weren't. Why weren't you? What could the people managing that situation have done differently to affect your engagement?

- Do you believe that cultivating engagement among your team members is, or is not, within your management power? If not, what needs to change? How can you bring about this change?

- Review the list of engagement suggestions. Do you agree with everything on the list? With what do you disagree? Why? What needs to happen for you to activate all the items on the list?

- How would resetting your management ability to engage people impact your professional life? Your personal life? Your other activities?

- What can you do immediately to reset and improve your management ability to engage people? What's stopping you?

3. Why You Have to Be Accountable to Your People

~

We must hold ourselves strictly accountable. We must provide the people with a vision of the future.
—**Barbara Jordan**, Former US Representative

~

To get the desired results, you need to be both responsible and accountable. You need to understand the *difference* between responsibility and accountability. And you need to be accountable both for and to your team.

In terms of people management, being accountable to those you manage will help you to get better results from them. Here's why. There is an important distinction between responsibility and accountability. When you're responsible, you are charged with causing something to happen or producing a specific result. Responsibility can exist before, during, and after actions are taken.

When you're accountable, you are answerable for justifying the actions taken, either by you or someone else, to meet a responsibility. Accountability exists only after actions have been taken.

I find lower productivity among teams where there are ambiguities and confusion over who is responsible for what, and who is accountable for what. This is why it's so important to provide written performance expectations to your team. By defining roles, every team member knows what they're supposed to do, where they fit into the process, who they report to, and who will be held accountable for their production and the production of the team.

In contrast, I find greater productivity among teams where each team member knows the specific results they are responsible for, the manager is responsible for both the aggregate team result and the way those results are achieved, and the manager is accountable to both those above him and the people being managed.

To reset your understanding of people management, be accountable to the people you manage. You can do this in the following ways:

1. **Communicate** with your team regularly and openly.
2. **Share information** with your team about how the total project is progressing, what obstacles exist, and how you are working on their behalf to make it as easy as possible for them to do their jobs and succeed.
3. **Maintain an open-door policy** so your team members feel comfortable coming to you to share information and get information and updates about what's going on.
4. **Tell your team when you made a mistake,** explain how it happened, and tell them what you're doing to fix it.

5. **Let your team know when you go to bat for them,** how things worked out, and how things are going to change, or why they aren't.

Being accountable to the team of people you manage *humanizes* you. It allows you to present a role model of how you want your team members to behave.

Being accountable to the people you manage is one of the most powerful ways to manage people to success.

The Great Management Reset: Why You Have to Be Accountable to Your Team

- Accountability can be daunting because it means you have to take ownership of your actions and possibly the actions of others as well. How can you make being accountable less daunting for yourself? How can you make being accountable less daunting for the people you manage? How will being accountable to the people you manage support the success of the team? How will being accountable to the people you manage make you a better manager?

- Do you believe that being accountable to the people you manage is, or is not, within your management power? If not, what needs to change? How can you bring about this change?

- Review the list of management accountability suggestions. Do you agree with everything on the list? With what do you disagree? Why? What needs to happen for you to activate all the items on the list?
- How would resetting your approach to management accountability impact your professional life? Your personal life? Your other activities?
- What can you do immediately to reset and improve your management in terms of being accountable to the people you manage? What's stopping you?

Task and Project Management

~

First, have a definite, clear practical goal. Second, have the necessary means to achieve your end. Third, adjust all your means to that end.

—**Aristotle**, Ancient philosopher

~

Your job as a manager is to control the resources available to you in pursuit of the successful achievement of a goal. Your goal could be an ongoing assignment, such as the management of a finance department, a classroom, or a family. Or your goal could be the execution of a finite task, such as the construction of a building, the production of a report, or accumulating enough money to send your kid to college.

Whatever the goal you are responsible for managing, you will improve your success rate if you perform the following steps of project and task management:

- Get absolutely clear and specific about the goal you are managing to achieve.
- Write a clear and specific step-by-step plan to manage toward the goal.
- Identify and organize your resources.
- Thin-slice the ultimate goal into measurable objectives and milestones so you can experience, announce, and celebrate progress.
- Establish reasonable deadlines for each objective and milestone.
- Get started. Deploy your resources.
- Communicate the clear and specific goal to the people you are managing. Do so in such a way that your people become enthusiastically engaged in the project and committed to its success. Repeat as necessary.
- Communicate your clear and specific goal achievement plan—including objectives, milestones,

and deadlines—to the people you are managing. Repeat as necessary.

- Communicate the clear and specific responsibility and accountability functions of the project to the people you are managing. Repeat as necessary.
- Put your plan in motion. Manage it (read: control it) through to achievement.

Simple, right? Figure out what you're supposed to do and then manage your resources to get it done. What could be easier?

Except that's not how things go. Anyone who's ever tried to manage anything knows that, in the real world, every possible obstacle that can present itself will do so, and at the most inopportune time. But hey, that's the challenge and fun of management.

Your responsibility is to be prepared for "scope creep" (changes in the specifics of the goal) and changes in your available resources. This means that no matter how foolproof you think your plan is, you must always have a backup plan.

So what's the best way to manage tasks and projects?

You'll be way ahead of the game if you reset your management approach so that you:

1. Know how to decide what to do and when to do it.
2. Know how to set realistic goals.
3. Understand the value of a backup plan.

4. How to Decide What to Do and When to Do It

~

What is important is seldom urgent, and what is urgent is seldom important.

—**Dwight D. Eisenhower**, US president

~

When it comes to managing tasks and projects, deciding what to do and when to do it can mean the difference between success and failure. Often the challenge in knowing what to do and when to do it is caused by confusion over what is urgent and what is important.

When I talk about something being urgent, I mean that it is screaming for your attention right now, in this very moment. When I talk about something being important, I mean that it will move you forward toward your ultimate goal. Tasks come in combinations of urgency and importance. Knowing how to prioritize among them is key in effective management.

For guidance, I refer to the Eisenhower Decision Matrix popularized by thought leader Stephen Covey in his book *The Seven Habits of Highly Effective People*. Covey's Eisenhower Decision Matrix divides tasks into four quadrants, or categories, based on their relative urgency and importance, as follows:

1. **Urgent and Important**

   These are tasks that demand immediate attention and also provide long-term progress toward the greater goal. Urgent and important tasks include deadlines, legitimate crises that really cannot wait, and problems that must be solved now to move forward.

2. **Not Urgent but Important**

   These are tasks that do not demand immediate attention, but do require ongoing attention because they move you toward your goal. For example, planning and plan execution may not be urgent because they can be done any time, but they are important to your progress and they must be done at some time.

3. **Urgent but Not Important**

   These are tasks that are nudging you for response right now but don't do anything to help your progress. Typically, urgent but not important tasks are interruptions in the here-and-now that show up while you're working on the things that are really important.

4. **Not Urgent and Not Important**

   These are typically procrastinations or distractions. Forget them. They're not helpful.

I'm suggesting that you reset your understanding of task and project management by focusing exclusively on categories

1 and 2 above (Urgent and Important, and Not Urgent but Important). You can manage to do this in the following ways:

- Plan ahead so that you will meet your important deadlines without a sense of anxiety-ridden urgency.
- Assess the value of every action you can take in any moment, and make the decision that yields the greatest return on your investment of resources.
- If you've got two tasks that are tied in terms of urgency, importance, and value, first do the one that will take you the least time to complete. This will allow you to immediately cross one item off your list, giving you the time and endorphins you need to address the more demanding task. Don't stop until both tasks are done.

The Great Management Reset:
How to Decide What to Do and When to Do It

- Deciding what to do and when to do it is not always easy. Sometimes, no matter how you try to prioritize, you're still stuck and don't know which way to turn first. When that happens, do you know what resources are available to you for guidance (e.g., your supervisor)? Do you access your decision-making resources or try to make shot-in-the-dark decisions on your own? What advice would you give yourself to better manage the process of deciding what to do and when to do it?

- Do you believe that knowing what to do and when to do it is, or is not, within your management power? If not, what needs to change? How can you bring about this change?

- Review the discussion of the Eisenhower Decision Matrix. Do you agree with the way tasks are described and organized? With what do you disagree? Why? What needs to happen for you to achieve engagement and only address tasks that are Urgent and Important, or Not Urgent but Important?

- How would resetting your decision-making approach to your tasks, and when to do them, impact your professional life? Your personal life? Your other activities?

- What can you do immediately to reset and improve your management in terms of deciding what to do and when to do it? What's stopping you?

5. How to Set Realistic Goals

~

People with goals succeed because they know where they're going.

—Earl Nightingale, Radio legend
and personal development pioneer

~

I feel strongly about goal setting as an essential management tool. As an experienced manager, frankly I can't explain how it's possible to manage without practical, attainable goals. If you're not managing toward some specific result, then what are you doing with your time every day?

Here are two ways to set realistic goals.

1. **Be S.M.A.R.T. about realistic goal setting.**

   S.M.A.R.T. as an acronym for goal setting first appeared in a 1981 *Management Review* article by George Doran, Arthur Miller, and James Cunningham, in response to the concept of management by objective posited by Peter Drucker some thirty years earlier. Since then the acronym has assumed a variety of interpretations. Here's mine. S.M.A.R.T. realistic goals are:

   S: Specific, self-owned, and sustainable

   M: Measurable, manageable, and meaningful

   A: Appropriate, actionable, and attainable

   R: Relevant, resource based, and results oriented

   T: Time based, team focused, and trackable

2. **Set your goals by planning backwards.**

   The most productive way to establish a goal, and the objectives (steps) necessary to achieve it, is to work backwards from what you want to achieve to where you are right now. It works this way.

First, define what you ultimately want to accomplish.

Next, identify each of the milestones you will need to reach to accomplish your ultimate goal. In this step, you track backwards, milestone by milestone, until you get to the very first thing you will need to do to start moving forward and experience progress.

Then, break each milestone down into the resources you will need to organize, deploy, and manage in order to reach it.

Finally, write a plan of specific, individual actions that will lift you from level to level until you get to where you intend to be.

Reset your understanding of task and project management by managing the way you think about your ultimate goal and what it will take to get there. Be S.M.A.R.T. about realistic goal setting, and set your goals by planning backwards from where you want to end up to where you're starting from.

The Great Management Reset: How to Set Realistic Goals

- Realistic goal setting is a prerequisite for effective management. Realistic goal setting takes some forethought and work that can be made easier by activating effective techniques like S.M.A.R.T. goal setting and backwards goal setting. How can you incorporate S.M.A.R.T. goal setting and backwards goal setting into your management toolbox? How will realistic goal setting make you a better manager?

- Do you believe that realistic goal setting is, or is not, within your management power? If not, what needs to change? How can you bring about this change?

- Review S.M.A.R.T. goal setting and backwards goal setting. Are these techniques you can use to establish realistic goals? If not, why not? What needs to happen for you to activate S.M.A.R.T. goal setting and backwards goal setting?

- How would resetting your approach to management goal setting impact your professional life? Your personal life? Your other activities?

- What can you do immediately to reset and improve your management in terms of realistic goal setting? What's stopping you?

6. Why You Need a Plan and a Backup Plan

~

Go make yourself a plan and be a shining light. Then make yourself a second plan, for neither will come right.

—**Bertolt Brecht**, Playwright
and creator of epic theater

~

Here's the deal with management plans. You have to have one, plus at least one backup, or you aren't going to succeed.

If you fail to plan how you will manage to achieve your goal, you're most likely not going to achieve it. (If by some quirk of fate you do achieve your goal without a plan, you certainly won't deserve any credit for it.)

Having a written management plan gives you the following management advantages:

- A management plan defines what you expect to happen and how you expect it to happen.
- By articulating what and how you expect it to happen, your management plan gives you a specific purpose and direction.
- By having a specific purpose and direction, you exclude all other purposes and directions, thus isolating the resources and activities necessary for success.
- By isolating the resources and activities necessary for success, you minimize distractions and hone your focus.
- By minimizing distractions and honing your focus, you can make decisions based exclusively on reaching the end goal you are managing toward.
- By making decisions based exclusively on reaching the end goal, you are able to manage (control) and

measure standards of performance every step of the way.

- By measuring standards of performance every step of the way, you can adjust your plan moment to moment and guide your resources where you need them to go.

- By guiding your resources where you need them to go, your resources and you will ultimately arrive at a result that is close to, or better than, what you expected. That rarely happens without a plan to get you there.

So you must have a management plan. You also must have a backup plan (also called a contingency plan or Plan B).

Some people claim that having a backup plan dilutes the original plan. Experience has informed me that this objection to backup plans is irrelevant. So what if your original plan needs to be fine-tuned along the way? The overwhelming majority of plans live this way, constantly being evaluated, assessed, and adjusted. Look at it this way: You can't manage unless you're flexible. Your plans can't succeed unless they are flexible as well. Besides, the goal isn't what's changing—just the way you reach it.

Reset your understanding of task and project management by embracing planning and backup planning. You can do this in the following ways:

1. Accept that you always need a management plan. Always. Period.

2. Create the best, most comprehensive management plan you can. Then consider all the possible variables and come up with at least one backup plan—just in case life decides to have a little fun with you along the way to your management success.

The Great Management Reset: Why You Need a Plan and a Backup Plan

- Having an articulated management plan and a backup management plan is a requirement for your management success. How do you feel about creating an articulated management plan along with a workable backup plan? Are you concerned about the level of effort you'll need to invest in creating your management plan and backup plan? What level of effort will you need to invest down the road if you don't have a plan and a backup plan? How can you incorporate management planning and backup planning into your management toolbox? How will management planning and backup planning make you a better manager?

- Do you believe that effective management planning and backup planning is, or is not, within your management power? If not, what needs to change? How can you bring about this change?

- Do you accept the necessity of having both a management plan and a backup management plan? If not, why not? What needs to happen for you to acknowledge and accept the importance of management planning and backup planning?
- How would resetting your approach to management planning impact your professional life? Your personal life? Your other activities?
- What can you do immediately to reset and improve your management planning and backup planning? What's stopping you?

Time Management

∾

Don't say you don't have enough time. You have exactly the same number of hours per day that were given to Helen Keller, Pasteur, Michelangelo, Mother Teresa, Leonardo da Vinci, ThomasJefferson, and Albert Einstein.

—**H. Jackson Brown Jr.**, Bestselling author,
Life's Little Instruction Book

∾

I n my introduction to "People Management," I said that people are your most valuable resource. In this section on "Time Management," I'm here to inform you that time is your most finite resource. You can always recruit more people, and as you'll see in my section on "Money Management," there are ways to stretch or increase your funding. But while you may be able to extend certain deadlines, you can never beg, borrow, steal, manufacture, or increase the amount of actual time you have. You know this is true because even if you are able to extend a deadline, the floodgates remain open and everything headed your way will rush in to consume the "extra" time you think you've been granted. In reality, there is no such thing as "extra" time. All you have is all you have.

This makes time your most precious resource. Fortunately, it is also the resource over which you personally can exert the greatest degree of control.

Here are five of my most effective ways to manage time:

1. **You have to gain absolute clarity about your goal right from the start.** Know what you're managing toward or you will waste an incredible amount of time feeling around in the dark.

2. **Once you have clarity about your goal, start planning immediately.** Write a plan and a backup plan (as discussed in my section on "Task and Project Management"). Calendar deadlines and create timelines. Organize a workable action list that you refer to, modify, and update on a regular basis. While all this requires an up-front

investment of time, it will save you a ton compared to the time you will waste without these roadmaps to guide you.

3. **Delegate to your team.** You have been graced with some number of people who can support you. Engage them, deploy them, and utilize them toward the goal.

4. **Master how to prioritize your tasks and your attention.** Refer to the Eisenhower Decision Matrix in my section on "Task and Project Management" to help you.

5. **Keep the lines of communication open in all directions.** Make regular reports to those above you so they can give you feedback on your direction, and make regular reports to your team so they can make the best use of their own time.

So what's the best way to approach time management?

I think you'll be way ahead of the game if you reset your management approach so that you:

- Understand how to manage deadlines.
- Understand the importance of to-do lists and action lists.
- Understand how to manage time so you have enough time to do your own work.

7. How to Manage Deadlines

~

I love deadlines. I like the whooshing sound they make as they fly by.

      —**Douglas Adams**, Comic, and creator of
        A Hitchhiker's Guide to the Galaxy

~

My most important message about deadlines is this: You need to manage deadlines so they don't manage you.

Since there are almost always repercussions for failing to meet a deadline, here are ten thoughts about deadlines to keep you managing in the right direction.

1. **Your deadline exists because someone is depending on you.** You don't like it when others let you down. Don't let them down.

2. **Deadlines keep you on track and moving forward.** Meet a deadline and you have managed to get to your goal. You may now move on to your next productive task.

3. **Deadlines present the opportunity to sharpen your people management, task and project management, and time management**. They give you the chance to prove yourself as a reliable

individual. And they have the potential to be the gateway to new opportunities for yourself—if you make them on time.

4. **To manage toward your deadline, use what you know about the difference between urgent and important tasks**. Refer to the section on "Task and Project Management."

5. **With deadlines: under promise to over deliver.** If you can determine your own deadline, be smart and build in as much of a margin as the situation will allow. This way you give yourself the time you reasonably need to produce the result or product. And if you can deliver before the deadline, then you become a hero.

6. **Divide the deadline into specific milestones and plot them on your calendar**. This will keep you focused and productive.

7. **Identify your resources, engage your people, and start.** Don't wait until everything falls into place. That rarely happens, and you're wasting time while it doesn't.

8. **Be willing to put in the time necessary to meet the deadline.** If this means early mornings, late nights, or weekends, so be it. (But manage your best so it doesn't.)

9. **Decide whether 80 percent delivered by deadline is better than 100 percent delivered late.**

10. **If you must be late, advise the person who is waiting for you as soon as you know.** Agree on when you can deliver, and stick to that deadline without fail.

Reset your understanding of time management by grasping the nuances of deadline management. You can manage to do this in the following ways.

1. Accept the deadline you're working toward is important.
2. Get started right away, and work in milestone increments to deliver on time.
3. Under promise and over deliver if you can. But if you're going to cross the deadline, adult up, tell the truth, set a new goal, and manage toward it for success.

The Great Management Reset: How to Manage Deadlines

•   Deadlines are often the bane of management. With so many ongoing tasks and projects, deadlines serve to add pressure while consuming resources and attention. But deadlines can also represent management opportunities, as well as opportunities for you. Are you willing to look at deadlines not as negatives but as potential positives for your team and for yourself? If not, why not? What would have to happen for you to reset your approach to deadlines?

- Do you believe that deadline management is, or is not, within your management power? If not, what needs to change? How can you bring about this change?

- Review my list of ten ways to manage deadlines. Do you agree with the ideas presented? With what do you disagree? Why? What needs to happen for you to feel more confident about managing deadlines?

- How would resetting your deadline management impact your professional life? Your personal life? Your other activities?

- What can you do immediately to reset and improve your deadline management? What's stopping you?

8. Why You Need To-Do Lists and Action Lists

~

One of the secrets of getting more done is to make a TO DO List every day, keep it visible, and use it as a guide to action as you go through the day.

— **Jean de La Fontaine**, Seventeenth-century French poet and fabulist

~

I am fanatical about written to-do lists and written action lists.

To-do lists are for tasks. The ones I have found to be most successful are weekly, organized into the days of the week, with each day's tasks prioritized according to urgency and importance as presented in my section on "Project and Task Management." Tasks are checked off as they are accomplished. Remaining tasks are either deleted or moved to the next day, and the next day's tasks are reprioritized. This continues on a daily basis.

Action lists are for projects. An action list is a hybrid list and plan in the form of a spreadsheet. It contains not only the individual project tasks from the to-do list, but also columns to indicate the date each task was assigned, who is accountable for completing the task, the resources deployed for the task, the current task status, the task deadline, next steps, the actual date of task completion, and notes. Action lists are updated any time there is something to report. They provide a project history, a snapshot of the present project status, and the next steps toward project completion.

Here are four reasons I believe written to-do lists and written action lists are critical to successful management:

1. **You can't remember everything.** It's a fact: Your conscious mind can't hold more than three or four thoughts in its working memory. The rest don't make it through. So if you don't have a written to-do list and a written action list and you have more

than three or four things to get done, how are you remembering what they are?

2. **Organization is a fundamental element of management.** Written to-do lists and action lists keep you organized. It's not possible to be organized without them.

3. **Accountability is a byproduct of recordkeeping.** Recording who's responsible for what and who's accountable for what is a mandate for effective management. To-do lists inform responsibility, and action lists document accountability.

4. **Motivation is what keeps you moving forward.** Checking completed tasks off a written to-do list and documenting project progress on a written action list provides motivation to keep on keeping on.

Reset your understanding of time management by writing and referring to to-do lists and action lists. You can manage to do this in the following ways:

1. Accept that you can't remember everything that needs to be done or was done. Written to-do lists and action lists eliminate the stress, futility, and frustration of trying to carry everything around in your head.

2. Recognize that to-do lists and action lists are critical instruments of organization.

3. Document and track responsibilities and accountabilities. Written to-do lists and written action lists are the tools to do this.

4. Stay motivated through the accomplishment of your tasks and plans as you check off completed tasks and clarify your next management steps.

The Great Management Reset: Why You Need To-Do Lists and Action Lists

- Right now, off the top of your head, without looking at your existing lists or at the papers all over your workspace, write a list of all the tasks you need to accomplish in the next three days. Now write an action list of all the projects you're working on, including the individual project tasks from the to-do list, the date each task was assigned, who is accountable for completing the task, the resources deployed for the task, the current task status, the task deadline, next steps, the actual date of task completion, and notes. Now check your lists against your existing tasks, plans, and lists for accuracy and to ensure there were no omissions. What's that you say? You forgot to include some tasks on your to-do list and your action list? If that's the case, this exercise has served two purposes. First, it got you to acknowledge that you can't possibly keep everything you need to do in your head. And second, it got you to write a to-do list and an action list. Now keep it up.

- Do you believe that writing and referring to to-do lists and action lists are, or are not, within your management power? If not, what needs to change? How can you bring about this change?

- Review my four reasons for why I'm so fanatical about to-do lists and action lists. Do you agree with the facts presented? With what do you disagree? Why? What needs to happen for you to immediately engage with maintaining a to-do list and action lists?

- How would resetting your approach to to-do lists and action lists impact your professional life? Your personal life? Your other activities?

- What can you do immediately to reset and improve your management through to-do lists and action lists? What's stopping you?

9. How to Have Time to Do Your Own Work

∾

Decide what you want, decide what you are willing to exchange for it. Establish your priorities and go to work.
—**H. L. Hunt**, Texas oil tycoon and political activist

∾

Management is really a balancing act. As a manager, your job is to identify, organize, deploy, and control your resources to achieve your goal. In addition to these imperatives, your management responsibility also includes tasks and assignments that only you, as the manager, can perform. These can include personnel-related tasks, attending meetings, finance-related tasks, attending meetings, reporting-related tasks, attending meetings, a host of other tasks, plus attending meetings. (I address the issue of meetings in the upcoming section on "Communication Management.")

As I see it, the challenge is how to manage your identification, organization, deployment, and control functions and still have time to address your own only-you-can-make-it-happen tasks and assignments. Here are nine ways to manage in order to have the time you need to do your own work:

1. **Write those to-do lists and action lists.** They will remind you what needs to be done.
2. **Prioritize your tasks according to their urgency and importance.** This will keep your tasks in the proper order.
3. **Ignore distractions and overcome procrastination.** This will keep you moving in the right direction.
4. **Learn to say no when the task you are being asked to perform does not contribute to your goal.** This will eliminate time suck.

5. **Get your endorphin rush from real progress, not from wheel spinning or brink deadlines.** This will move you from a frenetic state to a healthier steady pace.

6. **FOCUS (Follow One Course Until Success).** Work on one task for one project at one time. When you're done, move on to the next task.

7. **Delegate.** That's what your team is for. This will free you to address what's really important while helping you to identify and groom the next generation.

8. **Take short breaks now and then.** Your body and your mind need time to refresh and renew. Walk around, go out, eat, or use the bathroom. You'll be more productive.

9. **Respect your own circadian cycle, your daily biological rhythm that dictates when you'll be most and least productive.** Use it to schedule tasks for optimal results.

Reset your approach to time management to ensure that you have enough time to address the tasks only you can perform. You can manage to do this in the following ways:

1. Prioritize your to-do lists and action lists, and don't accept additional assignments that don't move you toward your goal.

2. Actually be productive. Focus. And delegate.

3. Respect your own humanity. Give your body and your mind a chance to rest, and use your own circadian cycle to your own management advantage.

The Great Management Reset: How to Have Time to Do Your Own Work

- Time is all any of us have, and time is limited for all of us. If you don't have enough time to get your management work done, you need to assess three variables: How much work you have, how much time you have to do it, and how you're scheduling your work in the time you have. Using your to-do lists, your action lists, and the team you manage, how can you execute and/or reduce your own personal workload? If you genuinely can't fit everything you have to do into the time you have to do it, how can you discuss your time dilemma with your supervisor? What value do you put on getting your management tasks and projects completed, and how does that compare with the value you place on your own health and sanity?

- Do you believe that managing to ensure you have enough time to do your own work is, or is not, within your management power? If not, what needs to change? How can you bring about this change?

- Review my nine ways to have enough time to do your own work. Do you agree with the ideas presented? With what do you disagree? Why? What needs to happen for you to activate these strategies?
- How would resetting your approach to having enough time to do your own work impact your professional life? Your personal life? Your other activities?
- What can you do immediately to reset and improve your management by having enough time to do your own work? What's stopping you?

Money Management

~

It is not from the benevolence of the butcher, the brewer, or the baker that we expect our dinner, but from their regard to their own interest.

—**Adam Smith**, Scottish philosopher
and a pioneer of political economy

~

I f people are your most valuable management resource and time is your most precious management resource, then money is your most powerful management resource. Make no mistake, money paves the way and moves things forward faster, more smoothly, and more easily.

You know this is true in both business and in life. A lack of money and/or poor money management limits all possibilities. When you don't have the funding you need but you want to expand the limits of your possibilities, you need to invest people power and time in achieving the subgoal of securing the resource of money. This distracts from and delays the achievement of your ultimate goal.

On the other hand, the presence of necessary funding and the proper management of that money removes a stressor and provides the means toward your end.

No matter what goal you're managing toward, no matter whether you're responsible and accountable for managing your own money or any part of someone else's, successful money management is essential to your management success.

I have a sense that most rational people working and living in a capitalistic society understand the purpose and importance of money. So I am concerned by the failure of many otherwise intelligent people to grasp the importance of money management, and by their resistance to learning the skills that will allow them to manage money productively.

Here are six common challenges to money management you need to overcome to manage money successfully:

1. You don't know how much money you have to work with.
2. You bought into someone else's erroneous notion that money is a "don't ask/don't tell" topic.
3. You don't know how to make a budget, how to read a budget, and/or how to manage a budget.
4. You're afraid you're going to make a costly mistake.
5. You don't know how to use the money you have to generate more money.
6. You don't want to be perceived as greedy.

So what's the best way to approach money management?

I think you'll be way ahead of the game if you reset your management approach so that you:

- Understand why profitability must be your first priority.
- Understand how to maximize the value of the team you're managing.
- Understand how to manage on budget.

10. Why Profitability Must Be Your First Priority

~

If your goal is anything but profitability—if it's to be big, or to grow fast, or to become a technology leader— you'll hit problems.

—**Michael Porter**, Economist, researcher, Harvard professor, business author

~

Profit is what remains of income earned after all costs and expenses related to earning that income have been deducted. Profitability is the capacity to make a profit. When I say that profitability must be your first priority in money management, I mean that you need to manage toward the goal of maximizing profitability so that you can produce a profit.

Unless your goal is to lose money or just break even, when I say that profitability must be your first priority in money management, I also mean that it must be your first management priority overall.

Be careful. Don't misconstrue this to mean that I have no real interest in the human side of management or that I'm suggesting you do anything and everything to maximize profitability and profit. On the contrary. I am very engaged in the humanity of management, and I do not suggest that you do anything illegal or unethical.

Here's why I believe that managing toward profitability must be your number one management goal. Profitability, and the ongoing generation of profit, are what keep the whole thing going, whatever "the thing" may be. In business, an unprofitable enterprise cannot long survive. Likewise, in private life, those who are in control of their own money management know they need to manage their money so that it works for them, for their present and future needs and comfort. They manage their money profitably so they can support their lives with something left over after their expenses are paid. Without this attention to money management, there can only be limited satisfaction, if any, of present and future needs and comforts.

In my experience, the challenges to money management and managing toward profitability can be conquered. When they are, new vistas of possibility, opportunity, and profitability appear. Here are five ways to manage money successfully:

1. **Know your budget.** You need to know what money you're working with. If you don't know, access the appropriate individual who does know and find out.

2. **Learn the ins and outs of budgeting.** Learn how to create, read, and manage a budget.

3. **Always get the best value for your money.** If you have the responsibility or opportunity to spend the

money you're working with, research the market, solicit competitive bids, and manage toward getting the highest return on your investment.

4. **Manage lean.** Activate every way to make your efforts yield more with less.

5. **Don't worry about appearing greedy.** If you're managing someone else's money, it's not you in your role of manager who will appear greedy. And if it's your own money, who cares what other people think?

Reset your approach to money management so that managing toward profitability is your priority. You can manage to do this in the following ways:

1. Get a handle on how much money you're managing.
2. Learn everything you can about budgets in general and your budget specifically.
3. Maximize the use of the money you have to yield the greatest return.

The Great Management Reset: Why Profitability Must Be Your First Priority

• Money and money management is a "don't ask/ don't tell" proposition for many people. Gone are the days when elementary schools helped third-grade students open savings accounts at local banks. Relegated to the circular file are old lesson plans that informed high school home economics courses. The current and next generation of managers needs to actively search to learn about money management, budgeting, and lean operating. What challenges do you experience around money management at work, at home, or both? What can you do to overcome those challenges and master managing money toward profitability? When will you start?

- Do you believe that managing money toward profitability is, or is not, within your management power? If not, what needs to change? How can you bring about this change?

- Review my five ways to manage money toward profitability. Do you agree with the ideas presented? With what do you disagree? Why? What needs to happen for you to feel more confident about managing money toward profitability?

- How would resetting your approach to managing money toward profitability impact your professional life? Your personal life? Your other activities?

- What can you do immediately to reset and improve your money management by managing toward profitability? What's stopping you?

11. How to Maximize the Value of Your Management and Your Team

∽

The greatest danger a team faces isn't that it won't become successful, but that it will, and then cease to improve.
—**Mark Sanborn**, Business and
team-building leader and author

∽

Value is perceived worth in terms of importance and/or money. Higher value equals higher perceived worth. It is both possible and advisable to increase your own value, the value of your management, and the value of your team and its contributions to increase your perceived worth. In my opinion, managing lean—a concept pioneered by Henry Ford and later fine-tuned by Toyota Manufacturing—is an effective way to maximize your own value, the value of your management, and the value of your team.

Managing lean is the process of eliminating waste and unproductive systemic redundancies. The purpose of managing lean is to maximize the efficiency of the resources (people, time, and money) and the workflow that you manage. Here are six ways to manage lean:

1. **Make sure you're working toward the right goal.**
   Make sure it's a S.M.A.R.T. goal (as presented in

my section on "Task and Project Management"), and that it remains a desirable goal to manage toward and achieve.

2. **Manage toward your goal within the budget you have been given, participated in creating, or created.**

3. **Eliminate waste by managing to produce the greatest amount of product or service with the least expenditure of resources.** Bear in mind that managing to produce the greatest amount with the fewest resources eventually hits a point of diminishing returns. Therefore, managing toward profitability must be balanced with a focus on the humanity of the people who are performing the work, the continued efficiency of your training and equipment, and a reasonable expectation of what can be produced with the resources of time and money that have been provided.

4. **Continually evaluate and adjust your systems for maximum efficiency.** Just because "it's always been done this way" doesn't mean it has to continue to be done this way. If you see a way to improve system efficiency, use your management position to test your new and improved system, document its success, create a plan to introduce it, and then find a way to implement it.

5. **Deliver more than you have been charged with delivering.** In other words, over deliver.

6. **Become the go-to manager and team in one or more of the responsibility or task areas you manage.** This will enhance your value as a resource. (Of course, manage your time when others come to you for assistance, as they invariably will, when you are known to be the greater-value manager and team.)

Reset your approach to money management so that your value, and the value of the team you manage, are enhanced and increased. You can manage to do this in the following ways:

1. Take a new look at the goal you're managing toward and make sure it's still S.M.A.R.T. (sustainable, measurable, attainable, relevant, and trackable).
2. Eliminate waste and increase systemic efficiencies wherever possible.
3. Over deliver in terms of product or service, as well as expertise and accessibility.

The Great Management Reset: How to Maximize the Value of Your Management and Your Team

- Management is not a spectator sport. It is an active engagement. You may not be the ultimate decision maker, but you are in the hierarchical stratum that bridges the decision makers and the frontline workers. Your observations and recommendations for lean management are therefore valuable and valid. How can you define your observations and recommendations for lean management? How can you test them, document their results, create a plan to introduce them, and ultimately implement them? What challenges do you expect to encounter? What can you do to overcome those challenges? How will doing this maximize your value, and the value of your management and your team? When will you start?

- Do you believe that maximizing the value of your management and your team is, or is not, within your management power? If not, what needs to change? How can you bring about this change?

- Review my six ways to manage lean and maximize the value of your management and your team. Do you agree with the ideas presented? With what do you disagree? Why? What needs to happen for you to take action and maximize your value, and the value of your management and your team?

- How would resetting your approach to maximizing your value and the value of your management and your team impact your professional life? Your personal life? Your other activities?

- What can you do immediately to reset and improve your money management to maximize your own value and the value of your management and your team? What's stopping you?

12. How to Manage on Budget

∼

The cold, harsh reality is that we have to balance the budget.
—**Michael Bloomberg**, Billionaire entrepreneur, philanthropist, and three-term mayor of New York City

∼

Managing money within a budget is critical to money management success in both your business and personal life. If you consistently overspend on a management budget provided to you by your supervisor, someone else will likely replace you in your management position. No company can afford to indulge the undisciplined spending habits of an overzealous or financially undiligent manager. Similarly, if you overspend in your personal life, unpleasant and possibly dire consequences can ensue.

Conversely, if you demonstrate that you are able to manage money on budget—or better yet under budget— while still managing to produce high value—or better yet increased profitability—for the people you're accountable to, you will have at least enough, if not more, money to manage with. And you will be lauded.

Experience informs us that, short of the point of diminishing returns, there are always ways to cut expenses and/or increase productivity and revenue within a budget. Here are eight ways to successfully manage money on budget:

1. **Review every budget as soon as you get it to ensure that it is sufficient to your lean money management needs.** Although there are always ways to cut expenses and/or increase productivity within a budget, be mindful of that point of diminishing returns below which you cannot go and still manage to produce products or services of real value.

2. **Search for ways to reduce both variable and fixed costs.** Research and take advantage of bulk pricing and better pricing from alternative suppliers.

3. **Research and imitate the best practices of others in your situation who are managing on budget.**

4. **Maximize time management to maximize efficiency.** (Refer to my sections on "Task and Project Management" and "Time Management.")

5. **Encourage your team to generate ideas for cutting costs and generating more revenue.**

6. **Incur and carry as little debt as possible and maintain a spotless credit rating.**

7. **Over deliver in whatever way you can to increase perceived value and generate increased profitability.**

8. **Be financially accountable to yourself and to others.** Be able to justify your spending, cost cutting, and revenue-generating management through documentation and objective measurement.

Reset your approach to money management so that you manage on budget. You can manage to do this in the following ways:

1. Cut fixed and variable costs wherever possible.
2. Find out how others in your situation are managing on budget and do what they do.
3. Be financially accountable through documentation and measurement.

The Great Management Reset: How to Manage on Budget

- Managing on budget is a superior management competency that will serve you in both your professional and personal life. Enhancing your ability to recognize and minimize or eliminate waste and inefficiency will serve you in many ways. Even before you activate any of the suggestions presented in this section, think about the waste and inefficiency you experience every day, in every aspect of your life, and how it could be eliminated. For example, how could the coffee shop where you buy your morning cup be spending less while providing comparable products and services? What about your local supermarket? The school? What about at your job? And in your own home? By becoming aware of how lean management can be applied to management for profitability in everyday circumstances, you will naturally become a stronger money manager and a stronger manager overall.

- Do you believe that managing on budget is, or is not, within your management power? If not, what needs to change? How can you bring about this change?
- Review my eight ways to manage on budget. Do you agree with the ideas presented? With what do you disagree? Why? What needs to happen for you to take action and manage on budget?
- How would resetting your approach to managing on budget impact your professional life? Your personal life? Your other activities?
- What can you do immediately to reset and improve your money management so you manage on budget? What's stopping you?

COMMUNICATION MANAGEMENT

∽

The single biggest problem in communication is the illusion that it has taken place.

—**George Bernard Shaw**, Irish playwright and cofounder of the London School of Economics

∽

Throughout this book, I have advocated strongly for communicating with the people you manage and the people to whom you are accountable. It is unreasonable to expect to be able to manage successfully without communication. If the people involved in your tasks and projects don't know what you're doing and what they're expected to do, you will find yourself flying solo on a mission that really demands collaboration. A management situation without communication yields confusion, frustration, indecision, suspicion, resentment, and duplication of effort, among other unhappy results.

It's helpful to think of communication in terms of Who, What, When, Where, Why, and How. Consider these questions and respond to them from the perspective of the person or group that will be receiving the communication. Ask yourself:

- Who needs to know about this?
- What do they need to know?
- When do they need to know?
- Why do they need to know?
- How does this need to be communicated to them?

Everyone relies on communication to engage others and let them in on what has happened, what's happening now, and what's going to happen or needs to happen next. As a manager, you need to sharpen your communication skills to ensure that everyone is on the same page at the same time and that the activities for which you are responsible and accountable yield positive and forward-moving results.

As a manager, you also need to know how to receive information that others communicate to you, process the information, and manage toward the appropriate next step. Receiving information, evaluating it, and making a next-step decision is a big part of management. By sharing problems with others who can help you and by helping others who communicate their problems to you, you have the opportunity to use communication to make problems productive. That's a very good management skill to have.

One of the best ways to communicate with the people you manage and to whom you are accountable is to conduct meetings for that exact purpose. But beware. Managing a meeting is challenging. Unless your meeting participants believe that the meeting has purpose and is productive, they will communicate to you in a variety of ways that you have wasted their time. Conducting worthwhile meetings is critical to management success.

I think you'll be way ahead of the game if you reset your management approach so that you:

1. Understand how to communicate with the people you manage.
2. Understand how to make problems productive.
3. Understand how to conduct worthwhile meetings.

13. How to Communicate with the People You Manage

∽

You can have brilliant ideas, but if you can't get them across, your ideas won't get you anywhere.
—**Lido Anthony "Lee" Iacocca**, American
businessman and architect of the
greatest comeback in business history

∽

Communication can be tricky. The challenge is that your audience—the person or people on the receiving end of your communication—will process what you're trying to share through their own filters. This means you must be careful to ensure that the messages people receive are the messages you intended to send.

It has been reported that as many as 40 percent of people are not satisfied with the level of communication from their supervisors. Here are six important ways to make your communication as effective as possible in both your personal and professional life:

1. **Communicate honestly, specifically, thoroughly, directly, consistently, timely, and regularly.** Communicate candidly with your team members and your supervisors, who are looking to you for infor-

mation. Give them the details they need to understand your message and why you are communicating with them about it. Get to the point and tell it like it is. Communicate the same message, in the same effective way, to everyone. Communicate when people need to hear your message, not when it's most comfortable for you. And update your communications on a regular basis to keep your people in the know.

2. **Be objective and respectful.** Communicate the facts without emotion or personal attacks. Communicate in a way that demonstrates respect for your audience.

3. **Use the appropriate means of communication.** This can include face-to-face meetings, phone conversations, e-mail, electronic conferencing, bulletins and newsletters, and all other means of verbal and documented information transmittal.

4. **Facilitate two-way communication.** As a manager, you must not only relay information but also receive it. This means that your people must feel that the lines of communication are open and that they can come to you when they have information to share. When your people respond to your communication or come to you to share information, be an active listener so that you can grasp the message they are relaying as well.

5. **Praise in public, reprimand in private** (with a witness, as appropriate).

6. **Be a constructive communicator.** The purpose of communication in management is to move you and your team forward toward your stated goal. The way you communicate can have a tremendous impact on how the people you manage receive and respond to the message you are relaying. Construct your communications to be as productive as possible.

Reset your approach to communication so that you produce the management results you're after. You can manage to do this in the following ways:

1. Build respect and trust by communicating fully, timely, and appropriately with the people who need to receive your message.
2. Keep the lines of communication open so you can receive information as well as sharing it.
3. Be a constructive communicator. Use communication as a tool to move you forward toward your management goal.

The Great Management Reset: How to Communicate with the People You Manage

- Communication is among the most important management tools you can use, and also one of the most challenging. Your communication must be deliberate and skillful if you wish to produce your desired results. What communication-related task do you have in front of you right now? How can you utilize my six ways to communicate effectively to help you craft and execute a successful communication?

- Do you believe that communication management is, or is not, within your management power? If not, what needs to change? How can you bring about this change?

- Review my six ways to manage communication. Do you agree with the ideas presented? With what do you disagree? Why? What needs to happen for you to incorporate these communication management ideas into the way you communicate?

- How would resetting your approach to communication management impact your professional life? Your personal life? Your other activities?

- What can you do immediately to reset and improve your communication management? What's stopping you?

14. How to Make Problems Productive

∾

Good management is the art of making problems so interesting and their solutions so constructive that everyone wants to get to work and deal with them.

—**Paul Hawken**, Leading environmentalist

∾

A problem is a situation that causes concern for one reason or another and that must be resolved to restore equilibrium and move forward. I have included this information on how to make problems productive in this section on communication because problem solving is a function of management, and because proper and strategic communication is essential to management problem solving. As a manager, you can turn problem solving into a productive event that yields benefits beyond the immediate situation for you and your team, company, family, or group.

Here are five ways to use management communication to make problems productive:

1. **Recognize that, as the manager, you are responsible and accountable for solving the problems that occur within your realm of management.** Accept this charge and address each problem head-on. Nothing can be gained, and much can be lost, by failing to do this in the proper timeframe.

2. **Use the communication techniques in my prior section to engage your team and create an environment where your team members feel respected and empowered.** They will then be on your side and more likely to work with you willingly to solve the issue. You may find that, because of an open line of communication, one of your team members has the experience to solve the issue in a

way you had not known. Or, a team member may come up with a creative way to solve the problem you had not even thought of.

3. **Use your management communication skills to ask and seek answers to the following questions:**
   - What are the specifics of this situation?
   - Why do these specifics constitute a problem?
   - What caused this problem?
   - What would the ideal solution to this problem look like?
   - What is needed to effect a solution as close to the ideal solution as possible?

4. **Communicate regularly with your team and your supervisors to give them a status report and keep them apprised of your problem-solving process.**

5. **Communicate your process to others who can help you and who might be helped by your information.**

Reset your approach to managing problems so that you use communication to make problem solving optimally productive. You can manage to do this in the following ways:

1. Accept that problem solving is one of your management responsibilities.
2. Use communication to clearly define the problem and how it can be solved.

3. Incorporate strong and deliberate communication in the process of problem solving so that your actions are documented and your results are shared.

The Great Management Reset: How to Make Problems Productive

- Throughout this book, I have made reference to the fact that management is not always a smooth path to walk. When the road gets bumpy, it is because you are confronted with a problem. As a manager, one of your primary responsibilities is to address and solve the problems in your realm. You can try to go it alone, or you can be smart and activate management communication to rally your troops and get the solution you need to move forward. What problems are you confronting right now? How can you engage your team to assist you in solving the problem and achieving the most desirable result? When will you start?

- Do you believe that managing to make problems productive through communication is, or is not, within your management power? If not, what needs to change? How can you bring about this change?

- Review my five ways to use management communication to make problems productive. Do you agree with the ideas presented? With what do you disagree? Why? What needs to happen for you to incorporate these techniques into your management communication and problem-solving toolbox?

- How would resetting your approach to managing communication and problem solving impact your professional life? Your personal life? Your other activities?

- What can you do immediately to reset and improve your management communication and problem solving? What's stopping you?

15. How to Conduct Worthwhile Meetings

～

Whoever invented the meeting must have had Hollywood in mind. I think they should consider giving Oscars for meetings: Best Meeting of the Year, Best Supporting Meeting, Best Meeting Based on Material from Another Meeting.

—**William Goldman**, Academy
Award-winning screenwriter

～

In my section on "How to Have the Time to Do Your Own Work," I implied that meetings typically consume a great deal of management time. A common sentiment among management thought leaders today is that meetings are often irrelevant and unproductive. This may or may not be true, depending on what goes on at any given meeting.

I believe meetings are important to the process of management. It's much more strategic and time saving to hold a single informational meeting for everyone who needs that information than it is to speak separately with those individuals. That said, some meetings *are* more productive than others. Unproductive meetings suck time and breed resentment. Productive meetings move you forward toward your management goal. In other words, they're worth the time people spent in them.

Here are seven ways to manage meetings so they are productive and worthwhile:

1. **Determine and communicate the exact purpose of the meeting.** It could be for information sharing, problem solving, or to move a process forward. Whatever the purpose, people want to know what you expect to happen at the meeting and after.

2. **Prepare yourself and your meeting participants in advance of each meeting.** Demonstrate your respect for your meeting participants by sending a notice of meeting far enough in advance so people can schedule their time. Include with your notice of meeting an agenda and all the documents and data that participants will need to have read to come to the meeting informed and prepared.

3. **Manage what happens during the meeting.** Stay on point and don't allow distractions to derail the proceedings and waste time.

4. **Set a time limit on discussions, decision making, and the meeting start and end times.** Stick to those limits.

5. **Create a meeting environment of productivity and teamwork.** Nothing will be accomplished if your meeting participants feel that they are being reprimanded in public or made to feel unproductive.

6. **End your meeting with a call to action that engages participants and clearly defines their follow-up responsibilities and deadlines.**

7. **Keep a record of the meeting, including who was present and decisions made.** As soon as possible, circulate this record in the form of minutes and an action list to everyone who participated in the meeting.

Reset your approach to managing meetings so that they are productive and worthwhile. You can manage to do this in the following ways:

1. Manage every aspect of a meeting, including the reason for the meeting, who is participating, the length of the meeting, what goes on during the meeting, and the call to action at the end of the meeting.

2. Make the meeting a positive and productive event focused on next steps.

3. Keep good minutes of your meetings, including a record of participants, decisions, and deadlines.

The Great Management Reset: How to Conduct Worthwhile Meetings

- Meetings can be boring, acrimonious, and unproductive. Or, they can be engaging, team building, and highly productive events. It all comes down to how they are managed. If you are stuck in a bad meeting, observe how the meeting could have been managed differently to produce a more positive experience. If you are responsible for calling a meeting in the near future, determine the purpose of the meeting, who is to attend, what information you can send to participants in advance of the meeting to make it easier for them to participate, how long the meeting and each discussion in the meeting will be, and who is going to keep the minutes. What challenges have you experienced in meetings? How would you manage a bad meeting differently so that it can be productive and worthwhile and so that it moves your forward toward your goal? When will you start?

- Do you believe that managing meetings so they are worthwhile is, or is not, within your management power? If not, what needs to change? How can you bring about this change?

- Review my seven ways to manage worthwhile meetings. Do you agree with the ideas presented? With what do you disagree? Why? What needs to happen for you to manage so that your meetings are productive and worthwhile?

- How would resetting your approach to managing meetings impact your professional life? Your personal life? Your other activities?

- What can you do immediately to reset and improve your meeting management skills? What's stopping you?

Service Management

The concept of service has engaged thinkers in every age and in every discipline, from economics and business, to government and military, to psychology and sociology, to philosophy and religion. The question at the core of every service-related discussion is: What does it mean to be of service?

It's challenging to identify a single, definitive response to this question because service itself is intangible. You can't measure the actual use or value of service in the same way you evaluate a widget. Widgets are material and have a physical existence, each widget has a specific purpose, and each widget has a measurable trajectory of process, cost, and return on investment. Not so with service.

Service is a phenomenon. It's not a thing; it's an experience. It's the interaction in which one party is called upon to provide help or work to another party who receives and benefits from the help or work that was provided. (In economics, the consumers of services, such as management, accounting, and law, are typically called clients, whereas consumers of tangible goods are typically called customers.)

All of management is a service phenomenon. Its purpose is to control resources and deliver not a physical product but an experiential result.

In my discussion, the clients of your management service fall into three categories. The first are your supervisors who determined your management goal and are responsible for overseeing your management activities toward that goal. As the manager, you must serve this group to justify the very existence of management in the first place. Your second group of management clients are the members of your management team. As the manager, you must serve this group in order for the team to serve its purpose. Your third category of service consumers are the actual customers who purchase the product your organization produces or the actual clients who purchase a service your organization provides. As the manager, you must serve this population as well.

Whether you're offering services or material goods, the consumer will be either satisfied or not satisfied with what he has received. As the manager, it is your responsibility to ensure the client's satisfaction. To paraphrase Supreme Court Justice Potter Stewart, service may be difficult to define, but people know it when they get it—and they especially know it when they don't.

I think you'll be way ahead of the game if you reset your management approach so that you:

1. Understand how to deliver service to your supervisors.
2. Understand how to deliver service to your team.
3. Understand how to deliver service to your consumers.

16. How to Deliver Service to Your Supervisors

∼

Accomplishing the impossible means only that the boss will add it to your regular duties.

—**Doug Larson**, Syndicated columnist

∼

Understanding how to deliver service to your supervisor means understanding your role as a manager. You are the conduit between the ultimate decision maker who has identified your management goal and the resources you will control to achieve that goal. This is not to say that you are not a decision maker and a leader as well. You are, and I look at the relationship between leadership and management in a special chapter toward the end of this book.

But for my present discussion, I will take a narrow view of your role as a manager in relation to your supervisor in order to present what is expected of you in that relationship.

As I have stated, the people in your management sphere want you to make things easy for them. Here are six ways you can deliver service to your supervisor:

1. **Be the keeper of the goal.** Keep your eye on the goal your supervisor expects you to manage. You must be able to remind your supervisor of this goal, tactfully and appropriately, whenever something threatens to derail it.

2. **Become the communication liaison between your supervisor and your team.** Your supervisor doesn't want to have to explain things to you and then again to your team members. Getting your team on board and up to speed is your job. Let your supervisor see you communicating and sharing information effectively.

3. **Bring the solution.** If a problem arises that you can manage without your supervisor's input, go ahead and manage it yourself. That's what you're there for. If a problem arises that you can't manage without your supervisor's input, you must communicate this to your supervisor honestly and thoroughly, and you must also present at least two solutions to the problem. Your job is to manage. So manage.

4. **Be proactive in your supervisor's interest.** Get to know your supervisor and what he is likely to ask for next. Present it before it's even requested.

5. **Make your supervisor look better and smarter.** Supervisors favor those who make them look more competent and knowledgeable in their own jobs. So master the relationship dance. Trust me. This advice will serve you well.

6. **Be the role model.** Represent for your supervisor the worker model she wishes she could but will never be able to replicate. Evidence in all your work the qualities of punctuality, accuracy, organization, loyalty, performance, and professionalism.

Reset your approach to delivering service to your supervisor so that you make his or her life easier. You can manage to do this in the following ways:

1. Be the exclusive "go-to" for every aspect of the management assignment.
2. Be the proactive problem solver.
3. Be the role model your supervisor wants to see.

The Great Management Reset:
How to Deliver Service to Your Supervisors

- As a manager, you are a vital element in the activation and manifestation of a particular goal. Your supervisor may have come up with the goal, but if he were interested in performing the day to day that actually makes it happen, you would be out of a job. What challenges do you experience around delivering service to your supervisor? What can you do to overcome those challenges and master the delivery of service to your supervisor? When will you start?

- Do you believe that managing the service you deliver to your supervisor is, or is not, within your management power? If not, what needs to change? How can you bring about this change?

- Review my six ways to deliver service to your supervisor. Do you agree with the ideas presented? With what do you disagree? Why? What needs to happen for you to feel more confident about managing your relationship with your supervisor?

- How would resetting your approach to the service you deliver to your supervisor impact your professional life? Your personal life? Your other activities?
- What can you do immediately to reset and improve the service you deliver to your supervisor? What's stopping you?

17. How to Deliver Service to Your Team

◦

To work effectively as an agent of change, it is necessary to be able to connect with people different from oneself.

—**Beverly Daniel Tatum**, President of Spelman College

◦

Throughout this book, I have emphasized the importance of the relationship between you, the manager, and your team— the people you manage. I also have provided numerous ways through which you can manage for maximum productivity from your team.

In the upcoming closing chapter of this book, I will discuss the integral relationship between leadership and management.

In this, my present discussion about delivering service to your team, I reflect on management thinker and writer

Robert Greenleaf's concept of the servant-leader and apply it to my new model: the servant-manager.

My concept of the servant-manager requires you, the manager, to actively commit to serving your team (read: make it easy for them to be productive) so that they will be equipped and inspired to be optimally productive in pursuit of your management goal. Here are three ways you can deliver service to your team:

4. **Put yourself in their shoes.** To yield the most productive relationship with your team members, you need to know what they go through day in and day out. The best managers have firsthand experience performing the actual work their team members have been assigned to do. Only when you have this experience can you truly empathize with and understand the messages your team members are trying to communicate to you.

5. **Be open to the truth.** As with all relationships, the truth may be painful, but hiding from it is far worse. You can serve your team members best by welcoming information from them about what's really going on. By doing so, you will demonstrate your respect for them as well as for your quest for the best way to accomplish your goal.

6. **Embrace the role of mentor.** In your relationship with your team members, go beyond your role as

a motivational coach and become a mentor. As a mentor, you relate to each team member not just as a producer of results but also in terms of their individuality and humanity. You not only critique and hone their performance, but you also share your knowledge, experience, and vulnerabilities with them. In this way, they learn to trust and respect you. As a result, your team becomes a vital community and you all grow together.

Reset your approach to delivering service to your team so that you become the servant-manager. You can manage to do this in the following ways:

1. Have personal experience of the jobs your team members perform.
2. Encourage and welcome the truth from your team members.
3. Be a mentor to your team members.

The Great Management Reset: How to Deliver Service to Your Team

- The image of the manager as a stern taskmaster is gone. It has been replaced by a more humane, more interactive approach that encourages the manager to serve her team so that the team, in turn, will serve the manager and the management goal. What challenges do you experience when you think of being a more humane manager? What can you do to overcome those challenges and master managing your team through your own service to them? When will you start?

- Do you believe that delivering service to your team as a servant-manager is, or is not, within your management power? If not, what needs to change? How can you bring about this change?

- Review my ways to deliver service to your team. Do you agree with the ideas presented? With what do you disagree? Why? What needs to happen for you to feel more confident about delivering service to your team and being a servant-manager?

- How would resetting your approach to delivering service to your team impact your professional life? Your personal life? Your other activities?

- What can you do immediately to reset and improve the service you deliver to your team? What's stopping you?

18. How to Deliver Service to Your Consumers

~

If you're not serving the customer, your job is to be serving someone who is.

—**Jan Carlzon**, Past Chief Executive Officer of SAS Group

~

As a manager, the time will surely come when you must be accountable not only to your supervisor and your team but also to a consumer of the results you produce. In business, this is likely to be clients or customers. In your personal life, this is anyone affected by your performance or the performance of the people you are managing toward a goal.

In the same way that you must deliver service to your supervisor and your team, you also must commit yourself to delivering service to those I call your consumers. Here are four ways to deliver service to your consumers:

1. **Think like the ultimate consumer of your management would think.** Take a global view of your organization or situation. Consider not only the people who are directly impacted by your management, but also those who are indirectly affected by it (consumers). Think about what you would want as the ultimate consumer, and then do what you can in your own sphere of influence to bring about a better consumer experience.

2. **Respect the position of your consumer.** Your consumer is the recipient of the results of your management. If not for the consumer, you would ultimately have no reason to manage. Be open to your consumers' input, and be especially attentive to the problems they bring to you. By resolving those problems, you strengthen your position with

your consumer while simultaneously strengthening your own management skill.

3. **Be knowledgeable.** Satisfactory managers know about their own little corner of the world. Good managers master their own little corner of the world. But exceptional managers have knowledge of the larger universe in which their own little corner of the world is a part. Become knowledgeable about as many aspects of your organization or situation as you can, including and especially those outside your immediate area of management. This will serve you in service to consumers and also elevate your position among your supervisors and team members.

4. **Be the best part of your consumer's experience.** This means accepting ownership of a consumer's issue and seeing it through to its successful end. If a consumer reaches you, that consumer will perceive you as representative of the whole. Manage the situation and be an exceptional ambassador of your organization and a role model for your team.

Reset your approach to delivering service to your consumers so that they have the best possible consumer experience. You can manage to do this in the following ways:

1. Understand the consumer's position.
2. Be an information resource for the consumer.

3. Make sure the consumer is better off after interacting with you than he was before.

The Great Management Reset:
How to Deliver Service to Your Consumers

- Although you may never interact with the consumers of your management, they are all or part of the reason you are managing in the first place. If you project yourself into the consumer's position, what do you see? How can you make a positive difference in your consumers' experience? When will you start?

- Do you believe that delivering service to your consumer is, or is not, within your management power? If not, what needs to change? How can you bring about this change?

- Review my ways to deliver service to your consumer. Do you agree with the ideas presented? With what do you disagree? Why? What needs to happen for you to feel more confident about delivering service to your consumer?

- How would resetting your approach to delivering service to your consumer impact your professional life? Your personal life? Your other activities?

- What can you do immediately to reset and improve the service you deliver to your consumer? What's stopping you?

Reputation Management

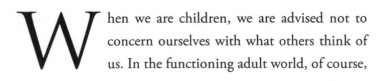

Trust, honesty, humility, transparency, and accountability are the building blocks of a positive reputation. Trust is the foundation
of any relationship.
　　　　—Mike Paul, "The Reputation Doctor"

W hen we are children, we are advised not to concern ourselves with what others think of us. In the functioning adult world, of course, we know that the way we are perceived by others has great potential for good or evil. We recognize that our reputation is a reflection of our values and ourselves; and we know that a good reputation is one of our most valuable assets and also one of our most fragile.

As a manager of anything—a business, a management team, a family, a sports club, or whatever—you are responsible and accountable for managing two primary reputations. The first is the reputation of the organization you represent. Because you are a manager of that organization, you are, by default, also a manager of that organization's reputation.

The second reputation you are responsible and accountable for managing is your own, in both your capacity as a manager and as a human being.

The benefits of cultivating a good reputation and being perceived positively by others are many. When all things are equal, a good reputation elevates you above your competition. It makes you a more desirable option because of the higher levels of trustworthiness, consistency, and transparency your good reputation implies.

When things are not equal, as often is the case, a good reputation can provide some degree of protection and defense against attacks from the outside. Additionally, a good reputation encourages you to operate consistently at a level that reinforces a higher standard of performance. It provides a role model for others. It allows you to bring yourself onto the playing field with confidence. And it attracts other people and new opportunities to you instead of repelling them, as a tarnished reputation will do.

As you know, communication technology makes it frighteningly easy to publicly attack, and even destroy, the reputation of an individual or an organization. You should know that it is far easier to build and maintain a positive reputation than it is to rebuild a damaged one.

Fortunately, there are ways to cultivate and protect a good reputation. And the same approach to reputation management is applicable to both organizations and individuals.

You'll be way ahead of the game if you reset your management approach so that you:

1. Understand why you need to articulate your values.
2. Understand why it's important to be consistent.
3. Understand how to enhance your own reputation.

19. Why You Need to Articulate Your Values

～

When your values are clear to you, making decisions becomes easier.

—Roy Disney, Senior executive of
The Walt Disney Company

～

Your values are your standards and principles of behavior. Because the values you believe in define your priorities, they provide direction for making decisions and taking action. In the end, the decisions and actions of every person and every organization reflect the values of that person and organization.

Since your reputation is based on others' perception of your actions, your values are the starting point of and contribute mightily to your reputation.

In my section on "How to Engage Your People," I encouraged you to articulate and document a Statement of Values for yourself and/or whatever group you manage. By doing so, you record the sustainable principles that guide your decision making and your actions. By following your documented values, you establish and reinforce your reputation.

Here are four ways to approach the articulation of your values and manage your reputation:

1. **Identify the values that identify you and/or your organization.** Clarify what you and/or your organization stand for and what performance promises you are making to your clients or customers. Examples of values that contribute to a positive reputation include honesty, courtesy, competence, proactivity, reliability, enthusiasm, and pride of product and performance.

2. **Ensure that the values you have identified support your management goal.** Your values must serve to move you forward toward your goal and they must express the ethics that drive your decision making. If your values do not support your management goal, then your values, your goal, or both, must be adjusted.

3. **Get values buy-in from your team members.** Every team member must demonstrate respect for the articulated values. When you and your team are out of values alignment, you must overcome two management challenges. The first is to communicate the values to your team. The second is to get them to internalize those values so that when they are faced with a dilemma they will know what values-based action is expected of them. This is the way to build and sustain a reputation.

4. **Communicate and document your values in a formal Statement of Values.** By doing this, you record the standards by which you intend to manage, and you provide a document you can access to resolve decision-making dilemmas.

Reset your approach to reputation management through values articulation. You can manage to do this in the following ways:

1. Identify your values and/or the values of your organization.
2. Ensure that your identified values support your management goal.
3. Articulate and document your Statement of Values for your management team.

The Great Management Reset: Why You Need to Articulate Your Values

- Your values define you and your reputation. For this reason, many people hesitate to document their values, preferring instead to temporarily adopt and espouse the values that are most popular or convenient at the moment. Yet values that stand the test of time and do not vary with whim or expediency are the ones that prove to be the most sustainable and most memorable to those considering your reputation. What challenges do you experience around identifying and articulating your values? What can you do to overcome those challenges and manage your reputation through articulated values? When will you start?
- Do you believe that reputation management through articulating management values is, or is not, within your management power? If not, what needs to change? How can you bring about this change?

- Review my suggestions for reputation management by determining your management values and achieving values buy-in among your team members. Do you agree with the ideas presented? With what do you disagree? Why? What needs to happen for you to manage your reputation through the articulation of your management values?

- How would resetting your approach to reputation management through values articulation impact your professional life? Your personal life? Your other activities?

- What can you do immediately to reset and improve your reputation management through articulated values? What's stopping you?

20. Why It's Important to Be Consistent

∾

If you don't stick to your values when they're being tested, they're not values; they're hobbies.

—**Jon Stewart**, Emmy Award-winning television producer, host of *The Daily Show*

∾

A good reputation is one of the most valuable assets you can possess and also one of the most fragile. Reputation is fragile because it can be attacked, damaged, and even destroyed, not only by forces outside of us, but also—and most tragically—by us.

You know this to be true. Just pick up any newspaper. I'm willing to wager that you will find at least two stories about individuals, or individuals acting on behalf of organizations, whose behavior has done serious, perhaps irreversible, damage to their own reputation and/or the reputation of the organization they represent. Individuals who have no one but themselves to blame for the negative perception others now hold of them. Individuals who failed to manage their reputation by acting in a manner inconsistent with their stated positive values.

For this reason, consistency is critical to managing reputation. Here are three ways to stay in alignment with your articulated positive values:

1. **Recognize that your articulated values are your pledge.** Respect the worth of your word as an individual, as a representative of an organization, and as a manager.

2. **Regularly review the alignment between your articulated values and your performance.** Values must be repeated and reinforced to become an internalized automatic compass. Take time every now and then to ensure that your decision making and your actions are in alignment with your stated values.

3. **Take immediate action when values and actions are out of alignment.** As the manager, it is your responsibility to bring decision making and actions into alignment with values. You can do this by assessing actions against the stated values to identify any disconnect, and then doing everything in your power to bring them together. When you are the one whose actions are out of alignment, you must manage yourself back into alignment. When a team member is the one whose actions are out of alignment, you in your capacity of manager must make a decision regarding how to achieve alignment, including the possibility that the team member may need to be jettisoned.

Reset your approach to reputation management by acting in a way that is consistent with your values. You can manage to do this in the following ways:

1. Internalize your stated values so that they act as your conscience and your guide.
2. Be mindful and conduct regular values and action-alignment assessments.
3. Take immediate action to bring values and actions into, or back into, alignment.

The Great Management Reset:
Why It's Important to Be Consistent

- Acting in ways that are consistent with our values is a challenge to every human being. If we let them, convenience, expediency, and negative temptations can easily throw us off our course. For this reason, many people hesitate to enforce their own positive values, preferring instead to make excuses for wrong decisions and questionable actions. While leniency and mercy are positive qualities in certain circumstances, the failure to adhere to fundamental, sustainable values, and/or to manage for such adherence from others, will mark you as weak, unreliable, and unpredictable. These are all undesirable characteristics for a manager. What challenges do you experience around making decisions and acting in ways consistent with your stated values? What can you do to overcome those challenges and manage in a way that is consistent with your stated values? When will you start?

- Do you believe that managing in a way that is consistent with your stated values is, or is not, within your management power? If not, what needs to change? How can you bring about this change?

- Review my ways to stay in alignment with your stated values. Do you agree with the ideas presented? With what do you disagree? Why? What needs to happen for you to manage by staying in alignment with your stated values?

- How would resetting your approach to reputation management through acting in alignment with your stated values impact your professional life? Your personal life? Your other activities?

- What can you do immediately to reset and improve your reputation management by making decisions and taking action in alignment with your stated values? What's stopping you?

21. How to Enhance Your Own Reputation

∾

It takes twenty years to build a reputation and five minutes to ruin it. If you think about that, you'll do things differently.

—**Warren Buffett**, American business magnate, investor, and philanthropist

∾

I cannot overemphasize the importance of a good reputation, both for yourself and for the organization you represent. A sustained positive reputation is the result of sustained positive action in alignment with your stated values.

Here are five ways to protect and enhance your reputation:

1. **Document and publicize the values that direct your decision making and actions.** People are more inclined to want to work with you, in whatever capacity, when they know what you stand for and what you won't stand for. By letting people know what your values are and that you intend to act in alignment with those values, you establish the standard, and the reputation, that people will expect from you and that you will expect from yourself.

2. **Make decisions and take actions in alignment with your stated values.** As I have stated, reputations are the direct result of actions. To protect and enhance your reputation and/or the reputation of the organization you represent, all of your decisions and actions must be in alignment with your stated values.

3. **Cultivate a reputation of service and participation.** Service to others, and participation in your immediate and extended communities, should be among your most important values. As a person or organization managing in alignment with positive values, you can protect and enhance your reputation by lending a hand and being an active member of your immediate and extended communities.

4. **Cultivate a reputation of approachability and transparency.** Typically, those individuals whose values and actions are subpar are the ones who

hide themselves for fear of being found out. You can protect and enhance your reputation by keeping an open-door policy, being thoroughly transparent, and being able to defend your decision making and actions through the articulation of your values.

5. **Cultivate a reputation of uprightness.** People who are upright behave in a consistently moral manner. They are trustworthy, honest, reliable, and forthcoming. Their commitment to these values does not waver and is not compromised in favor of an easy way out. You can protect and enhance your reputation by being an honorable person in all your actions and decision making.

Reset your approach to reputation management by being mindful of your own decisions and actions. You can manage to do this in the following ways:

1. Be specific and deliberate when you let people know what your values are.
2. Actively cultivate a reputation for service and transparency.
3. Ensure that your decisions and actions are above reproach.

The Great Management Reset:
How to Enhance Your Own Reputation

- Your reputation matters very much. A good reputation is to be prized, protected, and enhanced. What challenges do you experience around your reputation and how people view you? What can you do to overcome those challenges and master managing your reputation? When will you start?

- Do you believe that protecting and enhancing your own reputation is, or is not, within your management power? If not, what needs to change? How can you bring about this change?

- Review my five ways to manage your reputation. Do you agree with the ideas presented? With what do you disagree? Why? What needs to happen for you to take control and protect and enhance your own reputation?

- How would resetting your approach to reputation management by protecting and enhancing your own reputation impact your professional life? Your personal life? Your other activities?

- What can you do immediately to reset and improve your reputation management by protecting and enhancing your own reputation? What's stopping you?

CHANGE MANAGEMENT

❧

There is nothing more difficult to take in hand, more perilous to conduct, or more uncertain in its success, than to take the lead in the introduction of a new order of things.

—**Niccolo Machiavelli**, Renaissance historian, politician, philosopher, and author

❧

I f you're going to manage well, then you're going to have to manage change well.

In my discussion of Task and Project Management, I referred to "scope creep," or changes in the specifics of a goal. In my present discussion of Change Management, I am talking not only about scope creep but also about all interruptions in the status quo, and about the importance of knowing how to manage successfully through change and into the next "normal."

Make no mistake; managing change is a significant challenge. As if it weren't enough to manage the resources and variables that impact your management goal, the likelihood is great that one, some, many, or all of those resources and/or variables will present some kind of modification, adjustment, or difference that will impact one, some, many, or all of the others. And not just once, but on a frighteningly and often frustratingly regular basis. That's what change is all about.

Not only that, but change can and will come at you from a multitude of directions. It can be related to personnel, funding, time, or any of the other resources you need to achieve your management goal. It can be imposed on you and your team without your consultation or consent, generated by your team members, or even created by you. It can be the result of a natural occurrence or an engineered event, such as organizational growth or the installation of new leadership. It can be exciting and promising, as with a new product launch, or it can be daunting and depressing, as with a downsizing.

Change is the reason why flexibility and agility are so critical to effective management. It is also a major reason why I am so adamant about having at least one backup plan for every management project you undertake. (Again, I am not talking about changing the goal. I am talking about your management plan to reach the goal.)

As the manager, you must have an understanding of change as a phenomenon. You must know what happens to people and organizations in the face of change. You must know how to predict and prepare for change. And you must know how to rally your team members so they can undergo change and emerge unscathed and even more productive.

Good management during lull times is good. Good management during change times is mastery.

You'll be way ahead of the game if you reset your management approach so that you:

1. Understand what happens during change.
2. Understand how to plan for and execute change.
3. Understand how to get your team to embrace the next normal.

22. What Happens During Change

~

The world hates change, yet it is the only thing that has brought progress.
—**Charles Kettering**, American inventor, engineer, businessman, founder of Delco, head of research at General Motors, and holder of 186 patents

~

Around 500 BCE, the Greek philosopher Heraclitus observed that "Everything changes and nothing stands still." Yet although human beings have always been fascinated by change, the study of change as a management discipline is relatively recent. It is also essential to effective management.

Change is a deviation in the way things normally are. Because people drive change, and because people are affected by change, the study of change management is really an exploration of human behavior. For this reason, it is important to understand what happens to people, and by extension, to organizations, under changing conditions.

Many models have been posited to map the trajectory of change. In general, they follow a pattern that defines these stages of change for both individuals and groups:

- Shock, confusion
- Denial, rejection of reality
- Powerlessness, depression
- Experimentation, resetting
- Perspective, decision
- Acceptance, integration

As a manager responsible for managing change, here are four ways to move your people through these stages as smoothly as possible:

1. **Communication.** I cannot overemphasize the importance of letting people know about an upcoming change, how it's going to affect them, and what life is going to look like on the other side. In my experience, failure to communicate during a change event is the number-one reason most change initiatives fail.

2. **Community.** Divisiveness and a departure from focus on the ultimate goal are typical symptoms of a change event. For this reason, it is crucial to cultivate and maintain a sense of community and common purpose among your team members during change.

3. **Camaraderie.** Further to establishing the communal change experience, you as the manager must encourage a culture of helping, fellowship, and goodwill during change. This will alleviate some of the stress your team members are feeling.

4. **Coaching.** As the manager during change, it is your job to coach your team members so they get through the change process intact and motivated, and so that they are able to assume their new positions with competence and with the equipment they will need to be productive. By positioning yourself as their coach, you will generate a positive approach toward the coming new normal.

Reset your approach to change management by managing people's experience of the change. You can manage to do this in the following ways:

1. Communicate clearly, truthfully, and thoroughly through all stages of the change.
2. Cultivate a culture that focuses on one common goal.
3. Provide your team members with the resources they need to function post-change.

The Great Management Reset: What Happens During Change

- Change is frightening for many people, and most are resistant to change. Yet change is the only certainty, and nothing progresses without it. Think about your own change experiences. What challenges do you experience around change at work, at home, or both? What can you do to overcome those challenges and master change management? When will you start?

- Do you believe that managing change is, or is not, within your management power? If not, what needs to change? How can you bring about this change?

- Review my ways to manage your team members during change. Do you agree with the ideas presented? With what do you disagree? Why? What needs to happen for you to incorporate these strategies into your change management toolbox?

- How would resetting your approach to managing change impact your professional life? Your personal life? Your other activities?
- What can you do immediately to reset and improve your change management? What's stopping you?

23. How to Plan for and Execute Change

∾

It takes a lot of courage to release the familiar and seemingly secure, to embrace the new. But there is no real security in what is no longer meaningful. There is more security in the adventurous and exciting, for in movement there is life, and in change there is power.

—**Alan Cohen**, Owner of the Florida Panthers and founder of pharmaceutical companies

∾

As a manager, you will be expected to plan for and execute change. It doesn't matter where the change originates—whether from you, your supervisor, your team, or from a different source. It also doesn't matter whether what's changing is your stated management goal, or a resource, system, procedure, or policy that's related to your management goal. If the change involves you at all, you will be expected to manage it.

Here's the good news. The basic structure of a change management plan is happily similar to the management plan structure I discussed in my chapter on Task and Project Management. Here are nine steps to manage planning for and executing change:

1. **Identify where you are now and where the change will put you relative to your stated goal.** This will let you know what adjustments will need to be managed.

2. **Identify the resources you will need and have before, during, and after the change.** Change means things will be different, and that they will start becoming different as soon as you put your plan in play. Knowing what resources you will need and which ones you will have at any point during the change process will enable you to manage more efficiently.

3. **Set priorities and begin assembling your change management plan.** As with other types of management plans, write a clear and specific step-by-step plan to manage toward the change goal. Align the resources you will need and have, with the stages of the change, so you will be able to function at the highest possible level.

4. **Identify the measurable objective and milestones on the change path and establish deadlines for them.**

5. **Create and implement systems to support your change management plan and the resulting change.** Manage to ensure that the systems, policies, processes, and procedures affected by the change are able to keep pace with the change. Team members are more accepting of change when they can experience its evolution.

6. **Create one or more backup change management plans.** Contingency plans based on flexibility and agility are in greatest demand during change events.

7. **Execute your change management plan.** Put your plan in motion and manage it (read: control it) through to achievement.

8. **Set deadlines and keep action lists.** These will keep your change management plan on time and on track. (See my chapter on Time Management.)

9. **Communicate with your team and your supervisors on a consistent and thorough basis, cultivate a sense of community and camaraderie among everyone affected by the change, and be the coach who moves everyone forward toward the change goal.**

Reset your approach to manage planning and executing change. You can manage to do this in the following ways:

1. Get your arms around the change and adjust your current path to accommodate it.
2. Identify resources, set priorities, then write a change plan and a backup plan.
3. Implement your change management plan, complete with deadlines and action lists.

The Great Management Reset: How to Plan for and Execute Change

- Managing to plan for and execute change means that you accept the inevitability of the change and you intend to contribute a management plan and performance that will allow the change to take place as painlessly and seamlessly as possible. This is a tall order because change is often difficult for people, groups, and organizations. But as the manager, it is your job to manage so that an impending change can occur in an organized and ultimately successful manner. What challenges do you experience around planning for and executing change? What can you do to overcome those challenges and master planning for and executing change? When will you start?
- Do you believe that managing to plan for and execute change is, or is not, within your management power?

If not, what needs to change? How can you bring about this change?

- Review my nine ways for managing to plan for and execute change toward profitability. Do you agree with the ideas presented? With what do you disagree? Why? What needs to happen for you to feel more confident about managing to plan for and execute change?

- How would resetting your approach to managing to plan for and execute change impact your professional life? Your personal life? Your other activities?

- What can you do immediately to reset and improve your management to plan for and execute change? What's stopping you?

24. How to Get Your Team to Embrace the New Normal

∽

People don't resist change. They resist being changed.
—**Peter Senge**, American systems scientist

∽

As I have stated, change is a human phenomenon. It is also a human stressor, and when people are stressed they tend to be resistant. Your management goal is to relieve the stress, reduce the resistance, and encourage your team to embrace the new normal.

Here are seven ways to manage yourself and your team to embrace the change:

1. **Clarify for yourself how the change came about and how it will affect your team.** This is a preparatory step before you announce the change to your team. Get yourself into the decision loop, ideally as a participant but at least as an observer, and seek answers to the questions you expect your team will ask. In this way you can head off rumors and resentment and build acceptance and buy-in.

2. **Alert your team to all aspects of the change as early as possible.** You will lose your team's confidence if you allow change to blindside them. Advising them early about the change and how it will affect them will contribute to their trust.

3. **Involve your team in implementing the change.** While the larger change may be a foregone conclusion dictated by powers beyond your control, your team members are likely to have valuable insight into how the change can best be implemented on the front line. Reduce resistance and encourage engagement by giving your team members ownership of one or more aspects of the change implementation. In this way their focus will shift from resistance to participation.

4. **Be your team's change process resource.** Keep your door open and encourage your team members

to come to you with both their concerns and their suggestions. Also, keep them apprised of the milestones that have been reached in the change process and what's coming next. This will provide stability in a time of instability.

5. **Acknowledge the stages of change in your people.** You and your team members will invariably go through the stages of change I discussed in the section. What happens during change? Recognizing where your team members are along the change path will enable you to respond appropriately to them. It will also help to relieve your own stress when you realize that what your team members are expressing is part of their adjustment process.

6. **Be vigilant after the change.** Check in regularly with your team to ensure that they have embraced the change in their own responsibilities under the new structure. Recognize too that there will be some who can't or won't adapt to the change. An honest discussion will help to determine whether they can continue on your team.

7. **Communicate upward, too.** Keep your supervisor informed regarding your team's adjustment to change as well as your own. Your supervisors will appreciate that your management style includes concern for their own change-related stress.

Reset your approach to change management by managing toward engagement in the new normal. You can manage to do this in the following ways:

1. Become knowledgeable about the change and be a resource for your team.
2. Engage your team members by giving them ownership of some aspect of the change.
3. Demonstrate concern for your supervisor's and your own adaptation to the change.

The Great Management Reset: How to Get Your Team to Embrace the New Normal

- People typically embrace the status quo and resist change. But some changes are out of their control and others are inevitable. People have three choices in change situations: 1) They can embrace the change and define their role in it; 2) they can rail against the change and make life miserable for themselves and for others; or 3) they can simply walk away and move into a different, unrelated reality. Which of these is your typical response to change? If it's not to embrace the change and define your role in it, how has your response served you? What can you do to embrace change and move forward? What can you do to help the people you manage embrace change and move forward? When will you start?

- Do you believe that managing toward engagement during and after change is, or is not, within your management power? If not, what needs to change? How can you bring about this change?

- Review my ways to manage toward engagement during and after change. Do you agree with the ideas presented? With what do you disagree? Why? What needs to happen for you to feel more confident about managing toward engagement during and after change?

- How would resetting your approach to managing toward engagement during and after change? Your personal life? Your other activities?

- What can you do immediately to reset and improve your management toward engagement during and after change? What's stopping you?

SELF-MANAGEMENT

~

Mastering others is strength. Mastering yourself is true power.

—**Lao Tzu**, Ancient Chinese philosopher
and founder of Taoism

~

U p to this point I have focused on the management of external variables. I have discussed the management of people, tasks and projects, time, money, communication, service, reputation, and change.

121

Now it's time to look at self-management. By this I mean how you assess and control your own personal resources to achieve the goals you have set for yourself in every aspect of your life: your career and profession, your relationships, your physical health, your emotional well-being, your finances, your spiritual connection, and your personal development. The manner in which you manage, or discipline, yourself in each of these areas determines how you approach your own goals and impacts the results you attain.

Here are four ways you can take control and manage yourself for success:

1. **Define who you are and be consistent in your actions.** In my section on "Why You Need to Articulate Your Values," I said that values are your standards and principles of behavior. Your values define what you stand for and what you won't stand for. To achieve self-management, you must determine whether or not your values are consistent with each other and with your actions, or if they are situational and therefore sometimes confusing and counterproductive. The most successful self-managers in all walks of life know what they are about. They have taken stock of themselves, they are true to their values, they are willing to express their values, and their actions are in alignment with their values.

2. **Control your actions and be fully accountable for them.** It is not your thoughts, hopes, dreams, or desires that define you. Only your actions define you. To manage yourself successfully, you must be aware of your actions and accept that you are the one who performs them. As an adult, you must be accountable for your actions, and you must control them so they represent you as you wish to be represented.

3. **Understand that nothing comes from nothing and all results come from effort.** Thinking and wishing and hoping do not yield results. Only action and effort yield results. If you would manage yourself, then you must take action to move forward toward your goals. Nothing else will get you there.

4. **Accept and expand your humanity.** To manage yourself, you must accept the capacities, stressors, and limitations of being human and dedicate yourself to expanding those capacities, managing those stressors, and working through those limitations. Manage your mind and fill it with right information and inspiration. Manage your body and accept that it needs regular maintenance and repair to function optimally. Manage yourself for the results you wish to achieve.

Reset your approach to self-management to achieve your own goals. You can manage to do this in the following ways:

1. Define who you are, what your values are, and what you stand for.
2. Understand and manage the role of stress in your life.
3. Learn how to enjoy the moments that make up your life.

25. How to Take Stock of Yourself

〜

The individual who wants to reach the top in business must appreciate the might and force of habit. He must be quick to break those habits that can break him— and hasten to adopt those practices that will become the habits that help him achieve the success he desires.

—**J. Paul Getty**, American industrialist
and founder of Getty Oil

〜

As a manager of tasks and projects, you know that your resources are the means by which you achieve your goals. As a manager of yourself, your personal resources are likewise the means by which you achieve your personal goals.

More than a figure of speech, taking stock of yourself is the deliberate act of identifying your personal resources and their relationship to your personal goal. When you take stock of yourself, you look honestly and thoroughly at who you are and what you have, who you wish to be and what you wish to have, and what you have to do to get from here to there.

Taking stock of yourself entails an introspective five-step self-management process. This process will help to clarify your experiences and enable you to manage all aspects of your life more easily and more effectively.

Note this before you proceed. Unlike the management of an external goal in a public arena, this section of my book is dedicated to your internal management. No one else needs to participate in this section with you, and no one but you needs to know your process. That said, the five steps of self-management through taking stock of yourself are these:

1. **Identify your core values, the standards and principles that direct your behavior in the various aspects of your life.** Now is the time to really look at what you believe about yourself and about the world. If you're like most people, you will find more than one contradiction. The process of thinking about your values and determining whether or not they are congruent with each other is a major step toward truly knowing yourself.

2. **Assess where you are now and where you wish to be.** If every aspect of your life is exactly as you wish it to be, then there is no need to continue. If you're like most people, you will move on to the next step.

3. **Identify what you must do and the resources you need to get from where you are now to where you wish to be.** As a manager, apply the same planning to this step as you do to any other management task. The principles are exactly the same.

4. **Examine whether your core values support or undermine the actions you must take to get from where you are now to where you wish to be.** This is where the introspection really kicks in. In this step, you must either reconcile your own contradictions or determine that you can proceed despite them. I can tell you from experience, contradiction rarely contributes to progress.

5. **Decide and take action in response to the steps above.**

Reset your approach to self-management by taking stock of yourself. You can manage to do this in the following ways:

1. Identify who you really are and what you really want.
2. Assess what you have to do to get what you really want.
3. Decide and take action.

The Great Management Reset: How to Take Stock of Yourself

- Taking stock of oneself is often a scary experience. It means that you have to look honestly and thoroughly at your values and your actions and identify where contradictions are impeding your progress. What challenges do you experience around taking stock of yourself? What can you do to overcome those challenges and be honest and real with yourself? When will you start?

- Do you believe that taking stock of yourself to become who you wish to be is, or is not, within your management power? If not, what needs to change? How can you bring about this change?

- Review my five-step process for taking stock of yourself. Do you agree with the ideas presented? With what do you disagree? Why? What needs to happen for you to take stock of yourself to become who you wish to be?

- How would resetting your approach to self-management through taking stock of yourself impact your personal life? Your professional life? Your other activities?

- What can you do immediately to reset and improve your money management by managing toward profitability? What's stopping you?

26. How to Manage Stress

~

The greatest weapon against stress is our ability to choose one thought over another.
>   —**William James**, American philosopher
>   and psychologist

~

Stress is both a universal and an individual experience. It is universal because everyone experiences it. It is individual because what is stressful for one person is not necessarily stressful for another. When you feel stress, it is because some variable in your life is in conflict with another variable in your life. The result is an uncomfortable level of pressure or tension.

Stressors are everywhere and cannot be avoided. But it is possible to manage stress so that it doesn't get in the way of your forward progress. Here are five ways to manage stress:

1.   **Identify your stressors.** You can't manage anything until you know what it is you're managing. Are you a perfectionist? Do you have difficulty saying no when you really want to? Does it feel like there's too much to do and too little time? Perfectionism, people pleasing, and overscheduling are three of many common stressors. They each have a different

origin. Since not everything is stressful to you, naming what stresses you is an important step toward managing stress.

2. **Take control where you can and relinquish control where you can't.** Here invoke American theologian Reinhold Niebuhr's Serenity Prayer: "Grant me the serenity to accept the things I can't change, the courage to change the things I can, and the wisdom to know the difference." Live by this. It makes life much less stressful.

3. **Identify and adjust how you respond to stress.** Recognize what happens in your body and your mind when you're stressed. When you feel stress, go back to steps 1 and 2 above. For the things you can change, move on to number 4 below.

4. **Keep moving forward.** This is where the courage to change the things you can change comes in. Stress lingers when you dwell on the stressor variables instead of doing something about them. Great power and great stress relief occur in the moment of decision and taking action. Do not let stress distract or derail you. Stress is. Either accept it or remove it. Do not wallow in it.

5. **Protect yourself.** You can eliminate many of the negative physical and emotional consequences of stress by building protective barriers around your body and your mind. You do this by maintaining

your physical body and your mental equilibrium at all times. Exercise. Get enough sleep. Participate in regular recreation (read: re-creation). Maintain healthy relationships with family and friends. If you need to, seek medical or psychological help so stress does not rob you of your health, or worse, your life.

Reset your approach to stress management so that you, not the stressors, are in control. You can manage to do this in the following ways:

1. Recognize your stressors and how you respond to them.
2. Refuse to allow stress to thwart you.
3. Protect your body and your mind so they are always well defended against stress.

The Great Management Reset: How to Manage Stress

• Everybody experiences stress, but not in the same way. Some people actually court stress because it motivates them to action. Your relationship with the variables that stress you and how you respond to the stress you experience determine whether stress is a positive or negative experience for you. What challenges do you experience around managing stress at work, at home, or both? What can you do to overcome those challenges and master managing stress? When will you start?

- Do you believe that managing stressors and stress is, or is not, within your management power? If not, what needs to change? How can you bring about this change?

- Review my five ways to manage stress. Do you agree with the ideas presented? With what do you disagree? Why? What needs to happen for you to take control and manage the stressors and the stress in your life?

- How would resetting your approach to managing stress impact your personal life? Your professional life? Your other activities?

- What can you do immediately to reset and improve your stress management? What's stopping you?

27. How to Enjoy Yourself

∼

Summing up, it is clear the future holds great opportunities. It also holds pitfalls. The trick will be to avoid the pitfalls, seize the opportunities, and get back home by six o'clock.

—**Woody Allen**, American actor, filmmaker, musician, comedian, and playwright

∼

I want you to be a well-adjusted manager. This does not mean a manager with no problems or stress. That would be an oxymoron. If there were no problems or stress, there would be no need for management or a manager.

What I mean by well-adjusted manager is that I want you to be a productive, successful, and happy manager and person. I want you to actually enjoy your life, both when you're managing and when you're not. Here are six ways to manage to enjoy yourself:

1. **Identify and connect with what makes you happy.** If you would manage to enjoy yourself, you need to connect deeply and consistently with the people, experiences, and things that fill you will joy, contentment, and satisfaction. As long as what makes you happy is legal and falls on the good side of morality, I encourage you to manage your time, money, relationships, and all your resources so that you can identify and connect with the things that make you happy. Life is too short not to.

2. **Claim your time.** As I emphasized in my chapter on "Time Management," time is a finite resource. And I never know when my supply will run out. Even when you are working, you are in control of your time because you have willingly bartered it in exchange for some reward, such as a salary or some other form of payment. If you would manage to enjoy yourself,

I encourage you to remember that every moment you are alive belongs to you to do with what you wish. Claim as much of your own time for yourself as you can, and fill it with the people, experiences, and things you enjoy. Don't wait until you can't because then it will be too late.

3. **Get excited and expand yourself.** If you would manage to enjoy yourself, become more than you already are. Find something that excites you and expand yourself by immersing yourself in it.

4. **Relax and forget yourself.** On the other hand, if you would manage to enjoy yourself, dedicate some time to relaxing and forgetting about everything. Find the deep personal joy in just *being*. As a responsible manager and person, you will ultimately return to the things you wish to do. But for a brief while, be instead of do.

5. **Stop struggling.** Managing does not mean struggling. Managing means taking control and achieving. Let go of the notion that everything has to be hard. Decide what's really important to you and focus on that. Let the struggle go. Breathe and enjoy breathing.

6. **See it all—all of it—as a thrilling journey.** In the end, what you will leave is the story of your journey. Manage all of it so that you can honestly say, "I managed to enjoy my life."

Reset your approach to managing yourself so that you manage to enjoy your life. You can manage to do this in the following ways:

1. Figure out what you enjoy.
2. Pursue what you enjoy.
3. Enjoy every moment, no matter what.

The Great Management Reset: How to Enjoy Yourself

*   Some productive people feel guilty or nervous when they think about enjoying themselves. These people feel that if they're not working, they're wasting their time. Others feel exactly the opposite: that working is wasting valuable time. There is a happy medium and it arrives when you take control of your life and manage to enjoy yourself. What challenges do you experience when you think about managing to enjoy yourself at work, at home, or both? What can you do to overcome those challenges and master managing to enjoy yourself? When will you start?

*   Do you believe that managing to enjoy yourself is, or is not, within your management power? If not, what needs to change? How can you bring about this change?

- Review my six ways to enjoy yourself. Do you agree with the ideas presented? With what do you disagree? Why? What needs to happen for you to manage to enjoy yourself?

- How would resetting your approach to managing to enjoy yourself impact your personal life? Your professional life? Your other activities?

- What can you do immediately to reset and improve your management to enjoy yourself? What's stopping you?

Bonus Chapter #1
Leadership and Management

Many thought leaders assert that leadership and management are different disciplines, and that you are either a leader or a manager but not both.

I agree and I disagree.

I agree that leadership and management have different performance expectations. But I disagree strongly that you cannot be both a leader and a manager. In fact, I believe that you can and must be both.

Here's why.

It is widely accepted in the discourse of leadership and management that leaders paint in broad strokes and managers tend to the details. A common perspective is that leaders are the visionaries and managers are the technicians, leaders are the innovators and managers are the facilitators, leaders are the planners and managers are the executors. To paraphrase Peter Drucker, leaders do the right things and managers do the things right. So yes, leaders and managers have different performance expectations.

But it is my position that to be a superior manager, you must also be a leader.

Think of it this way. In my section on "How to Deliver Service to Your Supervisors," I said that as a manager you are the conduit between the ultimate decision maker who has identified your management goal and the resources you will control to achieve that goal. Once you have received your marching orders from the "leader," it falls to you, the manager, to identify, organize, deploy, and control your resources to achieve the "leader's" stated goal.

In other words, as the manager, you are expected to envision the path to goal achievement through resource management. You are expected to innovate efficiencies in the resources you control. You are expected to provide a plan that will yield the desired result. And then you are expected to control the resources and bring the desired result to reality.

I believe managers are, of necessity, leaders, and that you cannot manage effectively without also being a leader. As a manager, you must possess all the characteristics typically assigned to a leader. You must possess vision to plan and execute, and passion to carry you and your team through to task completion. You must be able to assess options and make decisions. You must understand how to assemble teams and influence people. You must control situations, relationships, systems, and processes to yield the product you have been engaged to produce.

The fact is, leaders don't need to know how to manage because that's what they rely on managers to do. But in my experience, and as I have shown throughout this book, managers must know how to lead to manage effectively.

And there is another way to look at the relationship between leadership and management as well.

When you as a manager master the science and art of management, if you wish you can then become a leader in the field of management. You can share your experiences, the wisdom you have gained from your experiences, and your perspectives on management innovations and improvements. Doing so, you will contribute to the growing field of management knowledge and help other upcoming managers to be stronger managers and leaders.

Just as I hope I have done for you.

BONUS CHAPTER #2
THE RHYTHM OF MANAGEMENT

L et me ask you a question—what unites the following people: President Thomas Jefferson, President Bill Clinton, Secretary of State Condoleeza Rice, astronaut Neil Armstrong, genius Albert Einstein, basketball legend Oscar Robertson, author Stephen King, billionaire businessman Bill Gates, and—sorry, but I couldn't resist— Larry Harmon, better known as Bozo the Clown, a TV clown personality who basically raised a generation.

To answer our question:

- Thomas Jefferson played cello, clavichord, and violin.
- Bill Clinton is an accomplished saxophone player who spent his summers developing his skills at a music program in the Ozarks.
- Condoleeza Rice dreamed of becoming a concert pianist.
- Neil Armstrong, the first man to walk on the moon, plays the baritone horn.
- Albert Einstein, Nobel Prize-winning physicist, played piano and violin.
- Cincinnati Royals and Milwaukee Bucks basketball player Oscar Robertson played the flute.
- Record-breaking author Stephen King plays guitar in the band Rock Bottom Remainders.
- Microsoft founder Bill Gates plays the trombone and founded the Microsoft Orchestra.
- And Larry Harmon, better known as Bozo the Clown, was not only a TV personality and shrewd businessman who produced and owned the Bozo the Clown franchise, he was also a percussionist who pursued music throughout his life.

All of these people reached the pinnacle of success in different disciplines. What unites them is not only their study of music but how they embraced music as part of everything they did. Nor are these isolated coincidences. The list of successful businesspeople, inventors, politicians, writers, scientists, and others who refer to the benefits and advantages of music in their lives goes on and on.

I have come to see more clearly the influence that music has had on me, and the true value that my music education has had in my life. Music was, and continues to be, my passion. And I graduated from college with the desire to become a professional musician.

Upon graduation, I took my viola and began studying for a master's degree in musicology. I became a teaching assistant while also taking private lessons and playing in various community orchestras. But I was not born into wealth, and because there were rent and bills to pay, I also took a part-time job as a billing clerk at a hospital.

You would think, as I did at the time, that being a billing clerk would prove uninspiring. But in hindsight, I now realize that a path was being shown to me.

Truth be told, I actually enjoyed the work. And apparently I did it well, because within two years I was appointed director of property management at Mt. Sinai Medical Center. My professional fate was sealed with that appointment, and I made the decision to focus my life's work on the business of real estate, all the while relying on music as my constant and loyal companion.

Since that time almost thirty years ago, I have founded seven real estate businesses that operate today in both New York and Florida, and I am proud to be able to provide jobs for more than fifteen hundred people.

For me to tell you that I focused my future in the real estate business, and then say that I did not abandon music, may seem at first to be inconsistent. But I will go to the grave thinking of myself as a musician first. And I have come to realize that everything I have achieved is intimately connected to how I understand the world as a musician. It is neither trite nor untrue for me to tell you that music has been the driving force behind every success I have had.

You may wonder how that can be. The answer to that question is at the core of my message to you. For now I will reveal to you what has been made clear to me: the hidden value of musical training.

Learning to Listen

Let's begin by talking about listening. Most people in the world hear. But I am often struck by their failure to really listen.

Musicians are schooled in the art of listening, in the ability to discern nuances, and to recognize and process subtle distinctions in shade and tone. The one word I heard most throughout my years of musical training was "listen."

As a successful businessperson, as a benefactor of various philanthropies, as a father, and especially as a husband, I can tell you that the most important skill I have honed in all my various endeavors is the ability to listen. Did I mention especially as a husband? Listening gives you an edge that those without this honed skill don't possess.

The Courage to Be Creative

French painter Henri Matisse said, "Creativity takes courage," and I couldn't agree more. As a student of music, you are constantly challenged to be creative, to take a piece of music and make it your own, and to create music where before there was none. Those who are so gifted sometimes don't realize how this ability sets them apart. But once you grasp the wonder of being a creative soul, you must realize how your creativity can be applied to everything you do.

Creativity is what directed me to develop and grow my businesses. To be an effective leader—be it at home or at work, at war or in peace—the ability to create, to bring about a reality that previously did not exist, and to own the result is what lends confidence and brilliance to decision making and leadership.

Primed for Performance

When I say performance, musicians immediately think of "musical performance." But life is full of performance opportunities. Speaking for myself, life as a business executive entails the demand to perform all the time.

Through their training, musicians gain an exceptional degree of performance confidence and poise. Approach a non-musician and ask them to present their innermost thoughts, feelings, or ideas to a group of strangers, and most would not be able to do so. But musicians are trained not only to perform before large groups of people, but to express their emotions through their instruments in front of total strangers.

The ability to perform, self-assured and with gusto, mistakes and missed notes and all, is an imperative for success in music, in business, and in life.

Capability to Conduct

Just as you must listen and be creative and perform, so you must conduct, in music and business and life.

As we go out into the world, each of us has countless chances to play the role of conductor. And if by design or fate you wind up in the business world, as I have, you will soon learn that the skill of conducting is essential for every effective businessperson and leader.

I still remember orchestra rehearsals with a favorite professor in college. Back then, the music building had just opened and the rehearsal room was in the basement. The only performance space on campus was the lobby of the administration building. But the limited facilities did not hinder this professor's ability to conduct, and I can still see his baton conjuring the magic of the music.

From that experience, I learned that the art of conducting cannot be altered by the environment. It must adapt and transcend circumstance and conditions. It demands the ability to get all members to play in unison, and to maximize each player's input by individual and section. It is the discipline to create each present moment—

while simultaneously looking moments ahead—in order to prepare for the future.

These are the same complex skill sets that are evident in the actions of every great leader. True leaders must recognize the potency and limitations of each player while leading and maintaining a focus on the future. These skills are the province of everyone who would lead, in music or business or life.

A Passionate Purpose

And so we come to passion.

Everything a musician strives for is defined by passion. Technicians can play notes as well as any computer program. But true musicians infuse passion into mere black dots on paper and convert those notes into a passion that can be experienced by every listener.

Passion for you and me is full engagement. It is the giving over of oneself totally to the experience. There can be no music without passion.

Likewise, there can be no success in any attempt without full engagement and the need to succeed, the drive to move through trying times, and the reluctance to ever walk away from anything without having given 100 percent. There can be no success in anything without passion.

For me, passion is the alpha and omega of everything I do. And I can tell you without hesitation that the passion within me was cultivated during my time of musical training. The passion that was seeded into me as a lover of music serves to make me passionate about my business endeavors as well. It is transmitted to every area of my life.

Music has inspired the great men and women of history, from the earliest time to today. That will never change.

As I bring this short chapter to a close, let me end with a personal anecdote. Although I love music in all its expressions, jazz has become my passion. I have attended the New Orleans JazzFest religiously for the past sixteen years. For the first few years, I always went with my wife or a friend. But I soon realized that while I could enjoy the music for hours on end, my guests got bored and thought I was completely insane.

My wife helped me to understand. And I quote her: "Yes, you are totally insane, having nothing to do with the music. The truth is, not everyone else hears what you hear." A friend of mine said something similar when I encouraged him to "listen to that bass line." His response? "I really can't pick it out."

But musicians will always be able to pick it out, to hear what others cannot hear. And that is precisely what sets us apart.

There will always be people who think that music should be played in the background. But not us. For us, music will always be at the forefront, in every moment of every day and night that we live.

If you love your music and live it, your music will surely guide you to success on whatever path you walk.

POST-READ MANAGEMENT
SELF-SURVEY

Below are the same twenty-seven statements from the Pre-read Management Self-Survey. As before, read each statement and then circle the number that best fits how well you agree with the statement. Add your total at the end. It is my intention that your score will be higher after you have read this book. Every improvement is a step forward toward your management mastery.

1. I understand what the people on my management team really want from me.

   1   2   3   4   5

2. I am able to engage the members of my management team so they are optimally productive.

   1   2   3   4   5

3. I am fully and openly accountable to the people on my management team.

   1   2   3   4   5

4. I am able to prioritize my tasks and projects easily and quickly.

   1   2   3   4   5

5. I know how to set realistic task and project management goals.

   1   2   3   4   5

6. I have a management plan and a backup plan for each task and project.

   1   2   3   4   5

7. I feel confident about meeting management deadlines.

   1   2   3   4   5

8. I use to-do lists and action lists to manage my time.

   1   2   3   4   5

9. I manage my time so that I have enough time to do my own work.

    1   2   3   4   5

10. My management plans target maximum profitability.

    1   2   3   4   5

11. I maximize the value of my management and my management team.

    1   2   3   4   5

12. I am able to deliver management tasks and projects on budget.

    1   2   3   4   5

13. I use communication effectively to keep my management team on track.

    1   2   3   4   5

14. I am able to make problems productive.

    1   2   3   4   5

15. I conduct worthwhile meetings.

    1   2   3   4   5

16. I deliver excellent management service to my supervisors.

    1   2   3   4   5

17. I deliver excellent management service to my management team members.

    1   2   3   4   5

18. I deliver excellent management service to the consumers (clients or customers) of my organization.

    1   2   3   4   5

19. I have clearly articulated my own values as a manager.

    1   2   3   4   5

20. I am consistent in the way I manage and in the results I achieve.

    1   2   3   4   5

21. I understand how to enhance my own reputation as a manager.

    1   2   3   4   5

22. I understand what happens to people and organizations during change.

    1   2   3   4   5

23. I know how to plan for and execute change.

    1   2   3   4   5

24. I know how to manage change so my management team members embrace the new normal.

    1   2   3   4   5

25. I take stock of myself regularly.

    1   2   3   4   5

26. I know how to manage stress in my own life.

    1   2   3   4   5

27. I manage my life so that I can enjoy myself.

    1   2   3   4   5

Post-read Management Self-Survey Total   _____

CONCLUSION FROM LESLIE

The unique techniques presented in this book will most definitely differ from those in other business books you might have read. That being said, my approach to management has a proven track record of providing the highest levels of both efficient and effective management services within any business setting, from casual to more traditional. Now that you have completed the pre-read and post-read surveys, you can track your growth as a manager. You are prepared to be a thought-leader in the next generation of great managers.

However, it is essential to remember that nothing in our world is stagnant; change is constant. The way we live day to day changes through the years. Our quality-of-life expectations differ from generation to generation. Even how we relate to one another is always evolving. What is trendy one day might not be acceptable in the future. Simply put, change is inevitable. As a result of this, our management methods must adjust accordingly to today's business environment. Buzzwords and fads just won't cut it. To remain stagnant is a grave mistake.

This book was designed to provide you with the various tools available to you as a manager. Like the tools in a carpenter's kit, these techniques are not "one size fits all." Flexibility and fluidity are key. Modify your management skills to fit your specific situation. Understand the value of each technique within this book, and work on matching the specific techniques with the individual employee.

Wishing you continued management success.

Leslie Kaminoff, CEO
lkaminoff@akam.com

About the Author

Leslie Kaminoff, RAM, NYARM, CMCA, LCAM, is founder and chief executive officer of AKAM Living Services Inc. (ALSI), which operates seven privately-held companies serving the real estate communities of metropolitan New York and South Florida.

Before founding AKAM Associates Inc., the ALSI flagship and one of the most innovative and highly respected residential management firms in the country, Leslie served as director of property management and assistant director of real estate for Mount Sinai Medical Center in New York City. Since founding AKAM in 1983, he has cultivated a reputation for himself and for the AKAM name as the premier provider of exceptional real estate services.

Under his guidance, AKAM Living Services has grown from the management of one twelve-unit apartment building to being a leader in the South Florida marketplace. Recipient of numerous industry awards over the past three decades, AKAM Associates has been recognized by The New York Building Managers Association as Management Company of the Year. *The Real Deal* real estate magazine has named AKAM Associates as one of the top five management companies and one of the top three privately-held management companies in metropolitan New York. In Florida, AKAM On-Site has been recognized twice by the *Florida Community Association Journal* as the Management Company of the Year in addition to winning the Go Green Property Award from the City of Aventura. AKAM-managed properties in both New York and South Florida consistently top lists of Best Places to Live.

A recognized leader dedicated to the professionalization of the residential real estate service industry, Leslie has served as an adjunct professor at New York University's Real Estate Institute and is a frequent host, keynote speaker, and panel member at industry seminars. He is the co-creator of the AKAM-RMP (Residential Management Professional) Training Program, New York's only credential-bearing proprietary training program for property managers sponsored by a management company. He is the author of numerous articles on residential real estate, co-author of the book *How to Choose the Right Management Company for Your*

Residential Property: A Decision-Maker's Guide, and author of the book *What to Expect from Your Property Manager*.

Leslie studied music at the State University of New York (SUNY) at Stony Brook and attended Long Island University. He is a graduate of the Ritz-Carlton Executive Leadership Program with concentrations in gold-star service and hospitality, values he has instilled in all of the ALSI companies. A generous benefactor of many philanthropic organizations, he is the recipient of the JAFCO (Jewish Adoption and Foster Care Options) Jacob's Ladder Award for Philanthropy. He plays classical viola and rock guitar. A devoted husband, father, and grandfather, Leslie Kaminoff divides his time among homes in Manhattan, The Hamptons, and South Florida.

In 2003, Leslie was the convocation speaker at Stony Brook University, discussing the relationship between music and business management. An edited version of his speech can be found in Bonus Chapter #2.

Printed in the USA
CPSIA information can be obtained
at www.ICGtesting.com
JSHW082338140824
68134JS00020B/1740

9 781630 479152